T0182699

I'M JUST A KID
WITH AN IEP

MY STORY

I needed who I am now when I was younger.

Now I will be that person for someone else.

JORDAN TOMA

I'm Just A Kid With An IEP

© 2022, Jordan Toma.

Print ISBN: 978-1-66783-9-974

eBook ISBN: 978-1-66783-9-981

This book is dedicated to every student

with a learning disability who has ever

worried about their success and their future.

You are all going to make it, I promise!

Jordan

SYNOPSIS

MY NAME IS JORDAN TOMA. I WROTE THIS BOOK because I believe that I have a powerful and inspiring message for young students with learning disabilities. This story highlights the struggles I endured from elementary school through high school. I am sending this message to students of all ages, parents, teachers, and anyone who has ever struggled in school or in life.

Today I am thirty-two years old and currently a financial advisor a Real-Estate investor. I own a home, and I have a beautiful wife, a two year old, two great dogs, and another business on the rise. While my life is now filled with blessings, it wasn't always this picturesque. I also have multiple learning disabilities that plagued me for the greater part of my life and made success seem impossible. I have been diagnosed with attention deficit hyperactivity disorder (ADHD), dyslexia, and a reading-comprehension learning disability.

My life as a learning-disabled individual has been a roller-coaster of emotions. I let these diagnoses control my life and diminish my confidence for my first eighteen years on this earth. I let my disabilities define me. Disability became a label stuck to my shirt every day, a permanent name tag. My name tag said, *I am not as smart as everyone else. I can't do it, this, anything.* The way I saw myself and how others saw me was a result of my experiences in school. Unfortunately, this inadequate identity grew roots into everything I did.

I felt helpless in class. I struggled to understand why I couldn't pick up information like everyone else. I remember sitting in class telling myself, *I am going to try really hard to understand everything in class today just like everyone else and be a normal student.* No matter how hard I wished it and how hard I tried, I couldn't grasp the material. I was made fun of because sometimes I had to have special lessons, specified classrooms, and learning accommodations. Other students, even so-called friends, called me dumb.

I let my learning disability and the way others saw me control me until I graduated from high school in 2008. Then, by the skin of my teeth, I was accepted into Centenary University on the terms that I complete a summer school program through the university called Step Ahead. At the time, I thought this program was a cruel punishment and yet another accommodation. However, during the course I quickly learned that it was changing my life. I moved into the university that summer filled with fear and anxiety. Despite my fears, I promised myself I was going to change. It was time to rip off the label that had plagued and limited me for so many years. With the help of Step Ahead and the power of my own will, I started building a foundation of confidence and belief in myself, brick by brick. It has delivered me to where I am today. Because I figured out a way to shed the skin of my disability, I feel the need to share my journey. I have an intense desire to help young students who can relate to my battles with learning disabilities. My desire is to help create the foundations of belief, confidence, and work ethic that you need to become the best you can be now, and not let anything ever get in your way.

For the full account of my inspirational story, please continue reading.

I needed the person who I am now to walk into my school when
I was a student. Now I will be that person for someone else.

—JORDAN TOMA

CONTENTS

CHAPTER 1:

CONFUSION AND MEDICATION

STARTING THIS STORY IS SO HARD. WRITING this book brings me back to when I was in school, when I was asked to write a paper or had an essay question on a test. I held the pencil between my fingers. What I wanted to say was in my head, but I just couldn't put it on paper. If I did manage to connect my brain to my fingers, the words I had written never seemed to make sense the way they did inside my head. I couldn't tell if it was just me, or if everyone had this problem. Nothing in school was clear to me; the information wasn't clear, am ability transfer my thoughts onto paper wasn't clear, my understanding of the letters of the alphabet wasn't even clear. I was just a kid with an individualized education plan (IEP). That's all I knew.

In sixth grade, I experienced my first anxiety attack when the school bus pulled up to my stop one morning. This continued to happen every morning when the school bus arrived to pick me up and take me to school. I saw the yellow bus coming around the corner with its flashing lights, and my heart would start beating like the grand finale during Fourth of July fireworks. I froze, my heart dropped, and I gripped the seat of my parents' car as hard as I could. My sister and brother jumped out and I held on for dear life! My dad screamed, "Jordan, you have to go to school!" I would start crying, and force him to turn around and go back down the street. It was like I could breathe again as soon as he turned the car back toward home.

I was scared to go to school because something didn't feel right. My body was telling me something.

Why? What was I so scared of? I used to ask myself that, trying to make sense of my fears, but I could never really pinpoint it.

I was young. I really didn't know what I was going through, but I sure didn't like it. I had great parents, though, and they would do anything to help me. I mean anything. My mother is a fighter. While she didn't fully understand it, she knew what was going on with me. She took me to every single top psychiatrist in New Jersey, New York, and Connecticut. Each doctor had a different approach. Sometimes they would keep me in the waiting room and bring my parents in to talk first. Thirty minutes later, they would bring me into the office as if they weren't just talking about me. *They must have not thought I was too smart after all,* I thought. Some offices had toys, some asked weird questions, and some just stared at me. We left, and when I got home there was always a different pill for me to take. They were new shapes, different colors, and had different effects. Every time I took one, I felt a little different. One pill knocked me unconscious; it was unreal. I would take it, and before I knew it, I was waking up.

I felt like a lab rat. They gave me the pills, and it was as if everyone in my life was observing me. My teachers reported their observations on how I was acting to my parents. After every doctor's visit, I always felt like my parents acted differently toward me and looked at me differently. Then there were new parenting techniques that they tried. Man, I got sick of taking all those pills every morning. One morning, I decided to do an experiment on myself. When my mom gave me my pill as usual, I put it under my tongue and spit it out as I walked to the car. I felt better, better than ever! I was still having a difficult time learning, but I felt good inside. The teachers started to tell my parents that they could see a difference in the new medicine I was on. Little did anyone know I hadn't been medicated in two weeks!

I loathed the doctors because of the way they talked about me to my parents, and I hated pills because I didn't like how they made me feel, like I wasn't myself. I was just a kid with an IEP, trying to figure out what was going on and how to make it better. To this day, I am still traumatized to take any type of pill because of the unwelcome feeling of not being myself that I felt so long ago has scarred me for life. I realized one thing at this point in my life: psychiatrists and medication couldn't fix me.

CHAPTER 2:

THE RESOURCE ROOM

EVERYONE KNEW ME AS ONE OF THE KIDS FROM
the resource room. Those of you who have an IEP or have a child with an
IEP are familiar with the term. For those of you who aren't familiar with
it, the resource room is a designated classroom for students who receive
accommodations. Every time the bell rings to indicate a classroom switch,
all students—resource and otherwise—take their seats in a regular classroom. Just as the teacher is about to start the lesson, another teacher comes
in and collects five or six students from the classroom. Sound humiliating?
I thought so. A public display of *You don't fit in here.* Other kids made fun
of the resource room and all of us in it. They would tell me, "Your tests are
easier," and, "That's the dumb room." The divide between the regular classroom and the resource room put a mental, social, and emotional divide
between the students. To me, it felt like there was an ocean between me and
the regular classroom that I was mentally unable to cross. Everyone acted as
if they were better than me, and I let them make me feel that way. This hurt.

While the resource room was a place I loathed due to the stigma that
encompassed it, it was a safe place. The regular classroom was a jungle, and
my experience with it left an impression that I will never forget. One day,
our resource room teacher was out for the day and there was no substitute
to cover for her, which meant that my fellow classmates and I had to join
the rest of the student body for the day in the regular classroom. I felt like a

little duck wading out into the ocean. The first subject was math. I sat at my desk filled with confusion and awe as the problems were presented to us. Letters and numbers coincided on the board. *That's algebra, right?* I didn't have the first clue what any of it meant; I might as well have been reading hieroglyphics. Then I witnessed what seemed like sorcery. Another student went up to the board and solved the problem. I was stunned. I said to myself, *How did he do that and when did he learn this?* The magic continued as student after student went up to the board and solved problem after problem. The teacher never called on me and I never raised my hand, but I prayed all the while that I wouldn't have to go up to the board.

The next subject was English. In the resource room, when it came to reading it was typical that we would read to ourselves, or the teacher would read to us. So, when the teacher in the mainstream classroom said that we were reading the current material out loud, I nearly fell out of my seat. *I wasn't ready for this! Didn't this teacher know I was scared to death? Were the other students with accommodations as petrified as I was?* I said to myself, *Of course the day my teacher isn't here I would get stuck with this guy.*

My heart felt like it was sprinting out of my chest, and I wanted to sprint out of that classroom—maybe I could occupy a safe stall in the bathroom—but I sat and waited for my turn with dread. Like dominos, one after another each student picked up where the previous one had left off. I counted the people ahead of me to project where I would have to pick up the reading. I scanned the paragraph to see if there were any hard words that I couldn't pronounce. I only had a few more people ahead of me, and I couldn't say the first word in my assigned section! I leaned over and asked the person next to me, "How do you say this word?" They told me, then shook their head in disbelief. Before I knew it, I was next.

The teacher called my name. I opened my mouth to begin, and right off the bat I mispronounced the first word. The girl next to me corrected me. As I continued my attempt to read, I mixed up brown and borrow. The know-it-all girl next to me was relentless; she corrected me again and again.

People laughed and shook their heads. It felt like one of those nightmares where the room goes dark and everyone in the background turns into jokers and clowns and they all laugh ferociously. I couldn't wait to be done with that paragraph. It felt like I was stumbling over those words for ten years, but it was only a minute or so. This experience shattered me. I was eaten alive in the jungle that day, and from there on out I prayed my resource room teacher would never leave us without a substitute again.

CHAPTER 3:

LETTING OTHERS MAKE ME BELIEVE I WAS DUMB (BIG MISTAKE)

THAT SAME YEAR, I HAD A CLASS WHERE THE teacher had a brilliant method for test preparation and review. The game was set up like the game show Jeopardy, and encompassed all the material from the last few weeks. So how do you think this teacher picked teams? In the most degrading way possible, how else? The teacher lined us all up against the chalkboard and picked four team captains. The captains then picked team members from the rest of the class, one by one. I dreaded this experience, because it was always the same. The last four picks came down to the four remaining resource room students. I remember being one of the last two picked and I said to myself, *I am the dumbest or second dumbest one in this class. No one wants me on their team.* I can still recall the painful expression on my resource room teacher's face as each one of her students sat anxiously, waiting to be picked for a team.

This was just another jab at my confidence. I let these students and this teacher manifest an image of me that was dumb, someone who was perpetually picked last. I revered those students who were team captains and those who were chosen first. I imagined what it must feel like to be smart and full of confidence. At this point in my life, being picked last from the group lined up at the chalkboard meant everything to me, and it defined me considerably. I put an enormous amount of stock into the idea that being rejected by my peers for a Jeopardy-style review meant something.

This humiliation was cultivated by my unoriginal teacher continued every week, and each time it left me feeling entirely inadequate. As an adult, I look back on this experience and recognize being the last pick in this scenario meant nothing. In fact, being picked last in general means squat! Your value and self worth cannot be placed in the hands of others. So, if you're feeling down on yourself because others aren't picking you or aren't recognizing you, shake it off. If I had held on to this experience, I never would have seen that it happened to me for a reason. I believe the reason was so that I would come back ten times stronger, to write this book for those of you who are feeling inadequate, like I did. There is a seed planted deep inside of you. Experiences like this don't decide who you really are, you decide who you are! That seed will sprout when you feed it with determination, test its limits, and silence the voices that make you feel small. If you keep that seed in the dark and starve it from the courage and resilience it needs, it will never blossom. Do you want to be the seed that blossoms or the seed that never sees the light?

CHAPTER 4:

THE TRANSITION

IT WAS ALWAYS MY DAD'S DREAM FOR MY brother and I to go to Private School, where he went to school. However, they didn't just take anyone. When my dad told me I would have to take an entrance test to determine whether I would get in or not, he looked worried. He looked more worried than I did, and I was very worried! The entry test was a typical essay setup. There were three possible questions you could get for your essay. They provided us with the possible essay questions before the exam, but it was still unknown which question I would have to answer on test day.

The night before the big test, my dad called me downstairs to help me with the essay questions. He said, "If you get this question, 'Why do you want to go to A Prep School?' write about how you want to get a great education." There was one problem. I couldn't spell education. I sat at our kitchen table, writing and rewriting the word education over and over again in hopes of retaining it. Again the next morning, my dad was quizzing me on how to spell education. Off we went to take the test. Man, I was anxious. My dad wished my brother and I good luck, and I headed into the building with the fear that I was about to let him down. As I sat there waiting, gripping my pencil with force and a sweaty palm, I looked around at all the other kids. I said to myself, *Wow, these kids look really smart.* They all had glasses on, they were dressed nicely, and I felt as if I stuck out like a sore thumb. I was certain my IEP tattoo was showing. They all looked self assured and prepared to crush this essay. I wished I were able to look that calm and confident. I wished I were able to feel that calm and confident. If those teachers only knew what was going on in my brain, they would have failed me on the spot.

Lo and behold, my essay question was, "Why do you want to go to this Prep?" This is the question I prepared for! I don't know if it was the nerves or my brain, but I forgot how to spell education. I was thinking, *Are you kidding me, Jordan? The one word you need for this essay, the basis of the question, and you can't remember how to spell it.* My brain failed me again.

One of the hardest things in the world for me is writing. So, being tasked with this essay was nothing short of difficult and on top of it, the essay needed to be handwritten. Generally, my handwriting is so horrific that I don't even know what I'm writing. So, there I am: I don't know how to spell education and I have horrible handwriting. I began to write anyway. I had so many great thoughts swirling through my mind, but they weren't translating on to paper. I really did want to get into this school. I wanted to make my father proud, and I figured I really could use a good education. I kept getting tripped up on the proper use of than and then, your and you're, and where to put the comma. By that point, I was completely overwhelmed by my inability to translate my thoughts, spell, or write legibly, and I just told myself, *Thank god my handwriting is so bad they won't be able to tell I couldn't spell one word correctly in this entire essay!* I stopped, stood up, and handed in my test. I was the first one done, and I couldn't tell if that was a good or bad sign.

Weeks later a letter arrived from this Prep School. To my complete surprise, I was accepted. I am clueless as to how, but I can tell you this, it wasn't because of my stellar essay.

CHAPTER 5:

HIGH SCHOOL WITH AN IEP

SO, I GOT IN TO THE PRIVATE SCHOOL. IT WAS MY first year as a high school student, and I was leaving behind my comfort zone. I had a chance to reinvent myself and to leave behind the image that everyone had of me. This was easier said than done, because I was scared, nervous, and unprepared. My biggest fear was that everyone was going know that I had an IEP and that I was just not smart. This sounds so sad when I think about it now; I really believed that. I truly felt that everyone was born with the gift of being smart and that God forgot about me. My mom tried her best to encourage me by saying, "You are smart. You just have to apply yourself." I had no idea at the time what she meant by this, because I felt like I was trying my best.

Day one of high school didn't go as planned. I couldn't find my first class! As I was looking for my class, I saw someone who looked like an upperclassman (more like a full-grown man). I showed him my schedule and asked, "Hey can tell me how to get here?"

He gave me directions, and off I went. As I was walking, I realized it was really far. That senior gave me the wrong directions on purpose to put me on the other side of the school! I weighed eighty-nine pounds, what was I going to do about it? I eventually found my way to class, late. This may seem like an unrelated insert to the story, but it kind of makes me think about how people and challenges can distract you and set you back. The important thing is that eventually you will make it, even if you get there late.

The first day of class, I sat there with clammy hands and thoughts spiraling around my restless brain. Thoughts like, *Does anyone know I have an IEP? Please don't call on me. I hope to God there isn't a read aloud. If I get called to go the board to write a problem or share my answer, I'm going to pretend like I don't understand so the teacher lets me stay in my chair.* Thankfully, I flew under the radar the whole day. For one day, I felt pretty normal. I felt like every other kid! I wondered how long I could keep up the charade. That week I had a pop quiz in science class. I failed it. I didn't get one answer correct. I remember the teacher saying to me "It's okay ... next time. That's only the first one."

After four pop quizzes, it was the same result: F, F, F, F. I may not be the best speller, but I got pretty good at understanding what F meant. Slowly, my camouflage started to fade. The teacher would call on me in class to read, and immediately my sweat glands went into hyperactivity. Most of the time, I couldn't speak. My throat did this awful thing where it would strangle my vocal cords. My worst nightmare was coming true.

My mom started to notice that I was really struggling. I guess it was the repetitive Fs I was bringing home and my general anxiety about school. So, my mother hired a tutor for me. Man, I've been through so many tutors you wouldn't believe it! At that point, we were four weeks into the school year and my English teacher assigned a paper, due the next week. I came home from school to greet my tutor and explained what I had due next week. We got started, and I was blown away by how intelligent this girl was. She sounded like a genius. I've never seen anybody come up with such great ideas and sentences. I started to feel cocky, like I was about to show this teacher what was up. Even though we were coming up with good material for my essay, I kept inhibiting my writing process with all of the errors I was making. The tutor noticed I kept stopping the flow with spelling errors so amiss that spell check couldn't even figure out the words. She said, "Let's switch seats. You tell me what you want to say and I'll type."

I had no problem with that, so I spewed out everything in my head and she made the words appear on the computer, looking and sounding pristine. She knew where to put every comma, every period, and where to indent; it was incredible.

Having been beat up the past few weeks grade wise, I couldn't wait to hand this paper in. I was proud of the work we came up with, and I knew that my teacher would be impressed. I handed in my paper, feeling like the man. A week later, our papers were graded. Five minutes before the bell rang, my teacher started calling people up to his podium one by one. I, as well as everyone else, could see the grades on the papers as the students walk by: A, B, B+, C, A-. My name was called and my paper has *See me,* in red. *What? See me?* I couldn't believe it. I was the only one with a see me. I walked back to my seat with my tail between my legs and waited for the rest of the class to leave. I felt alone again.

Everyone had left and moved on to their next class. I walked up to my teacher, who was standing at the podium with fire in his eyes. He looked at me and I felt his eyes burning through me as he said, "I am giving you an F on this paper because I do not believe you wrote it."

I replied positively, with my head high, "I did write it."

He said, "I don't believe you. Re-write it or it's an F in the grade book."

Tears pooled up in my eyes and my throat started to tighten like a snake around a mouse.

My first decent work, and this is what happened. This teacher assumed that because the work was done correctly and spelled correctly, I couldn't possibly have written it. It hurt to think that he didn't think I was capable of doing this. I did write that paper, they were my thoughts and words. I just didn't physically type it. I needed that tutor to help puts my thoughts on to paper in the proper format. I wanted to explain that to him, but I was too torn up and he made me feel like I did something wrong. He made me feel like I had something to be ashamed of. Talk about ripping the carpet out from under someone. Just when I thought I was going to be praised for my hard work, this was the result.

I went home angry. I told my parents I got another F and this time it was the tutor's fault. I was sad and discouraged, and the last thing I wanted to do was walk into that school in the morning.

I continued to see multiple tutors, but it seemed like nothing worked. I continued to show up to class, but never did anything right. Three months of school went by and I never did better than an F on any of my assignments or tests. I was on the battlefield now, constantly getting beaten up and beaten down. I failed everything that they threw at me. I was lower than I had ever been, and I finally had enough. I quit. I remember saying to myself, *If only I were born smart, I could be a part of the gifted and talented group and life would be so much easier.* Looking back, I realize that there are more gifts than the intelligence that gets you through school. Schools should really implement gifted and talented programs for students with gifts other than academics.

The next day I told my parents I was done and I didn't want to go to school there anymore. When you are young, every problem is the biggest problem in the world and this seemed like a planet-sized problem. I was so lost. I didn't have any faith in myself, and I had the image that I would never be a good student. Being the last person picked from that group at the chalkboard would always be who I was.

I was able to leave that school and rejoin public school, where things were familiar, where everyone knew me as one of the resource room kids. The Private Prep School gave me a break and allowed me to transfer to public school with all Ds instead of Fs. To be honest, it was the nicest thing they had done for me. After three months of failing, no teachers took the time to try and help me. It was clear that I wasn't leaving anything valuable behind.

CHAPTER 6:

SO I WAS BACK

THERE I WAS, BACK IN PUBLIC SCHOOL. I WAS relieved to embrace my old lifestyle. I was reunited with all of the other resource kids, all with their own issues and insecurities. Though we had our individual struggles, we all had one thing in common: we accepted that we weren't smart. This tied us together and I could breathe again, or at least with the normal anxiety level I had before private school.

As soon as I got back to public school, everything became a lot easier. There was no pressure back in my old domain, because no one there expected anything of me. I was put in classrooms with students who didn't care, and to be honest I didn't care either. One class I was in called study skills was the biggest joke. There was a teacher making an attempt to teach all of us who didn't care, and it was sad really. While the teacher attempted to teach, the students were acting like animals. Students were climbing on desks, getting into fights, sleeping, and blasting music in their headphones. I might not have cared about school at this point, but I still cared how everyone looked at me, how the others who weren't caged in study skills with the animals looked at me. I sat in that disaster of a classroom and watched students walking by with looks of dismay. I felt myself cringe each time I caught someone's eye, and I wanted to sit out of sight of the door so I couldn't be seen.

There was a stigma against the study-skills classes and the students in them. Teenagers are judgmental, we all know this. At the beginning of the semester, if someone from the study skills class was in a regular class, the other students would say it was an easy-level class. I always felt like everyone's eyes were on me in the regular classes, like I was making their class dumb by just being in it. I tried to push this thought out of my head. I was so insecure, always worrying about what everyone thought of me and what everyone thought about my brain. I wanted so badly to be regarded as someone with smarts. I wanted to erase those sneering looks off their faces and replace them with looks of admiration and envy for my intelligence. But how could I expect this of anyone else when I thought so little of myself? The truth was, it didn't matter what anyone thought of me at this point, or who, or if anyone even encouraged me. I didn't believe in myself; I was my own dark rain cloud.

CHAPTER 7:

GOD GAVE ME A LOT OF GIFTS, BUT WHY DIDN'T HE MAKE ME SMART?

THEY REQUIRED US TO TAKE A LANGUAGE CLASS in high school. I decided to take Spanish, because my mom spoke Spanish. I figured my chances of learning the language were better for some reason because she could speak it and could help me. I sat in Spanish class and I couldn't figure it out if my life depended on it! I wouldn't have known if they were speaking Greek, Mandarin, or Arabic. The teacher had us writing essays. If you have read this far, you have learned how great I am at essays, and until this point those were all in English. I remember trying so hard. Ultimately, I failed the class. I really needed to pass this class. I can still remember the teacher's name to this day, and I will never forget her face when she told me I had failed. I don't know why I was so worried about failing. I should have been used to it by then after my short stint in private school, but I really didn't want to fail this class too.

I didn't tell my parents about the F. I was very reluctant to tell them. I figured since my mom spoke Spanish, she would be more disappointed in me than usual. For the record, though, she wasn't Spanish and it was a silly thing to stress about. Stressing about excelling in a language in general was ridiculous. So, it was all over; I failed that quarter after I received that F.

After that day, I wrote a note to myself in my notebook. I wrote, "God, you gave me a lot of gifts, but why didn't you make me smart?" I knew that I had gifts. I knew it my heart that I hadn't been completely written off by God. I was a pretty decent wrestler, I made friends effortlessly, and I was born into an amazing and loving family (to name a few). In my mind though, there was one thing missing: I wasn't smart. I wanted to scream, "God, why am I not smart?! Why am I not capable?!" When you are young, your version of smart is compared to your peers. *Who aces the tests? Who does everyone go to for homework help? Who has the best and most intricate projects? Who gets picked first? Who is ranked at the top of the class?* I was none of these things, and it made me feel like I was floating at the bottom of the barrel. I frequently compared my abilities, or lack thereof, to my classmates. It wasn't healthy or productive. I didn't realize it at the time, as a child immersed in the education bubble, that smart meant a lot more than smart in school.

I had a math class called geometry two. I was so worked up and worried about that two behind the word geometry. Two meant I was leveling up, two looked scary and difficult. I am a financial advisor now, but math was and still is not my best subject. This just shows how much you really don't need this crap! To tell you the truth, unless you're planning on being a math teacher or an engineer, you really don't need any of it. As I wrote this book and reflected on geometry two, a particular situation came to mind. It was my first glimpse of success, and I missed it. I had this class with my buddy; he knew I was bad at math and I knew he was good at it, so I kept him close throughout the course.

We were a bit of a devious pair. Before every test, we would discuss our plan. We would get our test at the same time, and as he was taking it he would write down all the correct answers on his desk in pencil. When he was done, he would get up and hand in his test. Then he would sit back down and rewrite all the answers left in pencil on the desk into his agenda. So how did that help me? Given that I had an IEP I was given extra time to complete tests. So, I basically let the clock run out. Wrote stuff down, erased it. I looked out the window as if there were ideas and calculations running through my brain. When the class was over, my teacher would send the test to my study-skills class, where I was able to finish the exam on my own time. Before I went to study skills, my buddy would meet me and give me the answers from his agenda. I would take it to study skills and, well, you can figure out the rest at this point. It sounds pretty indecent, but boom, I passed! Just like that. I sold myself short because I didn't believe I could do it. Apparently, I wasn't the only one who didn't think I was capable of pulling off these recurrent passing grades.

This is where it got hairy. My teacher approached my study-skills teacher, who happened to be my wrestling coach at the time. She said to him, "Jordan takes his test down to you and comes back and gets a good grade. These grades are not typical of Jordan's work. I think you're giving him the answers. I don't think he is doing the work on his own."

Whoa, let me tell you my coach went nuts. He got so mad at her, because obviously that wasn't true. Little did he know I was cheating right under his nose, but it had nothing to do with him. I thought it was so funny that my math teacher went out of her way to assume this. Granted, she was correct, but it just showed how she didn't believe in me any more than I believed in myself. So, my teacher got slick. She said to me, "Next test, Jordan, you have to finish it right in front of me to prove to me you know this material." Oh, man, was I was in trouble. I ran home that day, called my mom, and said I needed a tutor ASAP. I desperately told her, "I need to pass this math test. My life is on the damn line! My coach is going to kill me and this lady teacher is going to think that he helped me." Not only was I scared for myself, but now I had gotten my coach into my mess. My mother had never seen me so serious about school or passing a test.

My vigilant mother called a math tutor straight away. I got dropped off, sat down, and started really focusing on what the heck she was teaching me. I kept doing practice problems after practice problems until she told me I knew it. I felt pretty good, but at that point in my life I had never really passed a test on my own. So, the nerves were welling up and my confidence was still relatively low. On the day of the test I was so nervous I felt like the teacher could see right through me, but I tried my hardest to play it cool and remember everything I had practiced with the tutor. While I was taking the test the teacher was grilling me, but I was making my way through the problems feeling good about the output. Given the circumstances, I walked away from that test feeling pretty darn confident. My brain was focused on the work, the numbers were making sense, and I wasn't feeling the usual helplessness that came with test taking.

The next morning when I walked into class my teacher was eyeing me up. She walked up to me and said, "I'm sorry. Good job. You passed!" *I passed? I know I'm bad at English, but did I just hear her right?* My first academic success accomplished all on my own. Right there, for the first time, I felt amazing. I had never felt so good before in my life. I was bounding with pride and relief. I can't figure out what happened though, and why I didn't keep this feeling going. It was a short-lived success. I went on for the rest of the year using my boy for all the answers. It is unfortunate that I didn't keep riding this wave. I proved to myself that day that I was smart enough and I was capable. I just had to work for it.

CHAPTER 8:

I WAS A WRESTLER

MY WHOLE LIFE I LOVED BASKETBALL. MY DREAM was to play in the NBA. One cool thing about being young is the naivete that comes with it: the ability to have a dream without borders. My dad is five foot seven and my mom is five foot five. I didn't have more than a 1 percent shot at playing in the NBA, but I really thought I could do it. My dreams were pretty crushed when I got cut from the basketball team. So, I tried my hand at wrestling. I didn't know one move. The only thing I knew about wrestling was that if I took someone down to the ground I got points. I tried out for the team and ended up making junior varsity (JV).

I remember my first JV tournament like it was yesterday. The match was in the back gym at school, my mom and dad came, and I was pumped up. I came running out on the mat when it was time for my match. I took the guy down as many times as I could and scored the maximum amount of points before the time ran out. I felt like a champ. I scored the most points in the entire tournament that day and took home first place. It was a crazy feeling for me, because it was the first time I was good at something naturally. Very little training, with a pretty clueless basis for the sport, but dang, I was good!

I discovered something I was naturally good at, a God-given gift. While I truly loved wrestling, I never became the wrestler that I could have been, that I should have been. I blew it, and it will haunt me forever. Throughout the years as a wrestler, I never tried as hard as I could have. I attribute this to my many years of not trying academically. By not trying my hardest academically, I mentally conditioned myself into the habit of having a poor work ethic. As I proved to myself with that one geometry two test, I was capable with hard work, repetition, and the right tools. Continuing to copy my buddy's work was just one example of not taking advantage of the talents that I had all along.

The saying, "Youth is wasted on the young," makes so much sense to me as an adult. Looking back, I realize that I let that the fact that I wasn't a good student decide what type of athlete I was going to be, what type of human I was going to be. I let my academic stumbles take over in other areas of my life. The ironic thing about my lack of work ethic is that I was always consumed with worry that I was never going to be successful. I truly thought the only way to gain success in this world was determined by how smart we are. I believed success was innate. I worried about this endlessly, and every night I prayed that life would bring success my way. Now I know that success isn't a God-given gift, and it doesn't flourish because you are smart. Success is bestowed upon those who work for it. I will forever kick myself for letting my poor work ethic and poor self-esteem bring me down on the wrestling mat. This could have been my first taste of success, and I let it slip away.

CHAPTER 9:

THE GREAT ESCAPE

I WAS JUST A KID IN HIGH SCHOOL, TRYING TO figure it out just like you are. I got in a little bit of trouble in those days, because I didn't really know what to do with myself. I used to skip school a lot and hang out at the diner; that was my spot. Looking back on these times of rebellion, I recognize some valuable character traits that I had, even at a young age. Pretty regularly, around 6:40 a.m., I would get the idea in my head to skip school. I would send a text out to all my buddies, *Skip school?!* They all would say, *No! Jordan! Stop, my parents are going to ground me.* I didn't take no for an answer or accept their excuses about being grounded.

When dealing with my friends and trying to convince them to rebel against school with me, I acted with persistence. I was obsessive, and did not take no for an answer. This is exactly how I am now when I am in pursuit of my goals. There was one particular day that I asked my friends to skip and they all said no, as usual. However, on this day I told them, *This day is different. Today we are going to do something big. Let's skip school and go to New York City!* They all said I was nuts. I replied with persistence, *It is happening!* I demanded they all meet me at Mike's house in an hour. My salesmanship convinced four of my friends, including my twin brother, to hop on a bus and head to New York City. It was an awesome day. Not only did we skip school, we managed to get ourselves to the city all by ourselves, and we got to see the magician David Blaine holding his breath underwater for a world record.

We also got robbed, since we were naïve fifteen-year-old kids trying to buy our way into places we shouldn't. Between all of us, we had forty five dollars on hand. We gave our money to a guy who said, "Wait here. I'll be back with wrist bands and we'll get you in." We waited at the door where he left us for an hour. Finally, the bunch of geniuses we were realized that he wasn't coming back, and that we had just been robbed.

The fun was over. As the sun started to go down, so did our chances of getting back into New Jersey without getting caught. It was getting late and all of our parents were looking for us at this point. We had only a few dollars to get back home. I turned on my salesman persona and convinced all of my friends not to answer their phones when their parents called. They listened, but it was not without consequence. We came home to a tornado of parental rage. None of us were allowed to see each other outside of school for months. On May 8, on our return to school, we all received in-school suspension for skipping. Well, that was a lot of fun because all of my friends and I were stuck in a room together all day. At least we had suspension to hang out together since our parents would have put a twenty-foot-high wall between us before they would let us be together again.

I learned a lot that day in the city. I learned that I did these types of things to escape the truth. I didn't want walk into the place that made me feel dumb day after day, so I did everything in my power to avoid it.

CHAPTER 10:

SAT

TYPICALLY, AS A STUDENT WITH AN IEP, YOU are used to getting test modifications. In middle school, they took us out of the room for the test and in high school the test layout was configured differently for us than for the rest of the students. For example, on a vocabulary test I'd get a word bank while the rest of the class didn't. On a history test, instead of four multiple-choice questions I would have two. For the SATs, the students with modifications were allotted two days to finish the test while the rest of the student body had a few hours. The time frame didn't change the fact that I didn't know the material, though. I was worried.

My parents were even more worried than I was. They hired an SAT tutor, pronto. Every day after school for weeks, I had to drive my brother and myself to the tutor's house after school. For one hour, one of us would sit upstairs with the tutor and the other one would take a practice test downstairs. It was torture. First, I couldn't sit still in general, so I could never sit down for an hour taking a test. Second, I couldn't understand even one question. I'm not kidding here, people. I didn't understand one thing. I grew pretty tired of this routine, and I diverted to my methods to avoiding actual learning.

After about a week of this crap, I started to check out. I abandoned my test and just walked around aimlessly downstairs while my brother was upstairs with the tutor. Then, I had a brilliant idea! I decided to go out onto her balcony and prank call her while she was tutoring my brother. I did that for an hour straight. I could hear my brother chuckling up a storm from downstairs. After forty-five minutes of pulling pranks on her, she started to call all of her neighbors looking for answers. When we left, my tutor and her neighbors were outside talking about some kids who were prank calling her, making speculations. With valuable time wasted in my rear view, my brother and I drove away laughing. That was two weeks of time wasted. I could have learned from this teacher. She could have helped me like the tutor who prepped me for that math test. I gave myself a zero on the SAT before I even tried. That is what I always did, and it was all I knew.

The day of the SATs, they put me in a special room with about five other kids just like me. We chatted among each other, exchanging hesitant glances. I remember someone saying, "Hey, we can't even cheat off each other because none of us are going to pass!"

I said, "I had a tutor for two weeks. I still have no idea what I'm doing, but you can cheat off me!" We all laughed in unison. If you haven't noticed it, when I couldn't physically avoid learning I used comedy.

The clock started counting down. I tried to answer the questions, but I didn't understand anything I was reading. I had heard somewhere that C is almost always the correct answer, so I relied heavily on the chances of this. I would pick C for ten questions in a row, then switch it up. I did that for the entire test, hoping to pull off the luckiest SAT score ever. After I walked away from that test I wasn't too concerned about my score, and I really never thought about I again until I needed to get into college.

Months later, I needed to access my scores for college applications. I will never forget it. I rummaged through all my stuff trying to find the paperwork. With no luck, I yelled downstairs to my dad and asked him if he had seen my score. He yelled back, "Very bad score." And that was it.

CHAPTER 11:

THE COLLEGE HUNT

I WAS PRETTY CLUELESS WHEN IT CAME TO COL-
lege preparation and everything that came with it. First, I didn't even know
what a major was. I just thought college was like a buffet: you went to college
and tried everything. If skipping school was a major, that would have been
mine. As I listened to my classmates talking about majors and reach schools,
I felt pretty left out. One day after school, I asked my mom and dad, "I'm
going to college, right?"

Enthusiastically they replied, "Yes, absolutely! You must go." This
encouraged me. My parents said yes, and everything was going to be fine.

On a Sunday night, my dad called me and my brother down to the
kitchen table. That was always an indication that something serious was
going to be discussed. He told us that starting next week we would be hit-
ting the road to check out colleges across New Jersey and Pennsylvania. At
this point, reality started to set in for me. I never excelled at school, I never
took it seriously enough to overcome my struggles, I blew off SAT prep, my
dad said my scores were very bad, and my GPA was low. Reality was that
this future seemed questionable. My dad's outlook on this trip was a little
intimidating. He seemed serious, which meant I needed to get serious too.

It was my dad's dream for his two sons to go to a good college of their
choice. Unfortunately, we didn't have that luxury. My dad had a big map with
all of our stops marked on it. First stop, Muhlenberg College. We walked in

the main doors, and it was nice. This place looked like the real deal. I said to myself, *I could never pass a class here.* All I could think about on our tour was whether or not I should tell this lady my GPA and SAT score. I had anxiety about wasting this woman's time.

When the tour was over, they gave us their application to fill out. There it was. The dreaded question, "What is your high school GPA?" I wrote down 1.7 and made up a bad score for my SAT. I showed my dad he said, "Oh my God. You can't put that on paper!" Trying not to make a scene, I replied with an unfavorable face and handed it in. My dad then walked into a room and shut the door as I sat outside. Ten minutes later he walked out, saying he thought I had a shot. The whole time, I was filled with anxiety trying to muddle through the idea of making it through college. *How could I make it on my own, and without modifications to boot?* Again, I gave myself an F before I ever tried. I failed before I tried so I failed to try, and that, my friend, is the worst thing you can ever do in your life.

If I could go back and tell my teenage self one thing, it would be, "Jordan, there is nothing in this world out of reach. We all have challenges. You aren't going to be good at everything; you just have to figure out what you are good at. You have to figure out what your gift is." I can tell you now that you must attempt everything. Keep trying, keep failing, and keep being scared. Dreaming big doesn't come without anxiety, and this will ultimately uncover what you are really made of and what you are here for.

Unfortunately, my teenage self didn't know the secrets I know now. The Jordan who was in the back seat of his dad's car admiring the colleges and the students they housed was completely out of confidence. My stomach roiled thinking about my inability to complete the college class work. I daydreamed during that car ride about what it would be like to be one of those students, strutting around campus and the college town. It seemed completely unrealistic to me that I could be one of those kids, wearing a t-shirt with the name of my college on it, a normal student. I had no belief in myself. I really believed that the inside of my dad's car, driving through campus, would be the closest I would get to a college experience.

We went to fourteen colleges throughout Pennsylvania and New Jersey. It was a long five days. Five days of driving, five days of walking around campuses, being embarrassed while filling out applications, and daydreaming about what could be. Every time we finished checking out a school, my dad would say, "I think you have a shot!" I really have to love my dad for this. He was so persistent, and he tried to keep my spirits up through the whole process. Driving through Pennsylvania somewhere, we passed Bucknell University.

My dad said, "This school right here, just wave at this one." Funny guy my dad.

Finally, we were back in New Jersey. My counselor and I sat down and talked about my week. He asked me about the schools I went to and inquired about how I felt. I told him, "I don't know. My GPA is a 1.7. I don't think I did well on the SATs. I really don't know."

He said, "Okay, well, let's just see what happens. Nothing we can do now but wait."

So I waited. Weeks went by, and the school year was coming an end. My first response came in the mail, finally. It was a decline. They would not accept me. I was told that if you get accepted to a school it will be a big packet. Mine were all small letters saying, "We cannot accept you at this time." I almost wanted the letters to say that, because I was so scared that if I did get in I wouldn't be able to get the schoolwork done at the level I needed to. I knew that if I did get accepted, college was going to be one of the hardest things I would ever have to do. The next letter came in the mail. I was denied. Thirteen letters trickled in over the weeks. Thirteen times I was denied. I started to get used to the feeling of rejection, but it still hurt nonetheless.

After the slew of rejections, I guess my mom thought it was time to intervene. She went to the high school to talk to the head of the child study team, some smart lady with a doctorate. I heard her later that night on the phone with the woman. I sat at the top of the stairs listening. She told my mom I should go to a two-year school because I would never make it through a four-year program. I felt like, *Damn, this person might be right. I let this person decide how my future would play out. How did she know what I could and could not do? Did she know my limitations? Did she know what I was capable of? How?* I sat there at the top of the stairs with my head on my knees. Half of me was pissed off that this lady was putting a ceiling on my capabilities, and half of me believed that she was right. I let someone who had no idea what I am made of tell me what I could do. I let her get into my head.

Here is the issue that I see with what I did. We all see this world out of our own eyes, but sometimes we let other people get in front of our vision. By letting other people's voices and opinions invade our thoughts, we diminish ourselves. We let these people take pieces away from our character. Ultimately, if we continue to let others' opinions diminish our shine, we inevitably become what they are envisioning. This only messes with our own vision, and I did this for way too long!

At this point, I had zero offers from schools, but there was one last school I was waiting on. I knew that this would be the one! My dad, uncle, and aunt all went to this school. I also thought that their donations would hold some leverage for me. It was a no brainer. I came home from school to my dad holding the letter. I opened it and read, "We cannot accept you at this time."

I looked up, completely stunned. I said to my dad, "Are you kidding me? You all went there. Uncle Jimmy wrote a letter for me!" My dad looked at me and said, "Jordan, you wouldn't have gotten in with a letter from the president of the United States." Funny guy, I told you. We both started laughing. Underneath my laughter, though, there was fear. Things were bleak for sure now. Jordan Toma: zero. College: fourteen. I felt like a loser. No one wanted me, not one school wanted to give me a chance. This was hard to swallow. Little did I know at the time, though, that a zero-and-fourteen losing streak was about to set me up for complete domination.

CHAPTER 12:

THE COME BACK

THE SCHOOL YEAR WAS WINDING DOWN, AND time was ticking away as far as getting into a school. With no acceptances, I was feeling lost. Things started to climb back up hill when my guidance counselor told me about a school that he thought might be promising. I got excited at this news. He told me it was still going to be a reach, but maybe there was a chance. I really wanted to go to school, but I couldn't shake that little monkey off my back that was too scared to try and fail. Despite these fears, we went on the website together and filled out the application. Additionally, I reached out to the wrestling coach from the college. I heard back from the coach before I heard back from the admissions office. The coach liked what I was doing with wrestling. Whatever he saw in me was based on pure talent, because I put very little effort into my wrestling. I didn't even want to wrestle in college, but I figured it might help my chances of getting in. I was hopeful when I heard back from the coach, but still I waited.

I waited nervously. About one week before high school graduation, I got a packet in the mail. I had been accepted into Centenary College, under one condition! They said with my grades and test scores so low, I must attend their Step Ahead Program. I didn't understand what was going on, and my joy was soon clipped.

I handed it to my mom and said, "Did I get in or what? I have to go to summer school?!" She congratulated me with great joy. I was pissed. I was graduating from high school in a week and now I had to go straight into summer school. I couldn't believe it. My mom tried to encourage me by telling me that this was a huge opportunity, I was being given a chance, and that the Step Ahead Program was going to do me well. I walked up to my room and screamed. I screamed in anger at having to go to summer school. I think there were underlying screams of fear, too. I was feeling a lot of emotions with the arrival of this packet.

My anger and fear turned into paranoia when I blamed my mom for this summer school scam. I was sure she had something to do with it. My seventeen-year-old self was completely convinced that my mother was trying to ruin my life. She told me of course that she had nothing to do with this, and that Centenary was just trying to ensure my success. My paranoia turned to bitterness as I thought about all the things that summer school would keep me from doing during those short months of freedom I was missing out on.

I was desperate not to have to go to summer school. I received a rare B on one of my final school assignments and I called the program director at Centenary, completely elated and hopeful that this grade would be proof that I didn't need to go to the Step Ahead program. When the program director picked up I said, "Hey, I got a B on one of my assignments and I'm good. Do I still need to come in the summer?"

He said, "Jordan, yes. That B doesn't mean you don't have to come. Your overall grades show that you need some further preparation before your college journey begins." My eyes watered with anger, and I slammed the phone down. I sat on my bed that hot June day and felt so much anger. I was angry at that program director and I was angry with my mother. I should have been mad at no one other than myself. After all, I was the architect of my future. I had a hard time getting into school because I had never tried. I missed out on my summer because I didn't try.

It was my final week as a high school student. I called my buddy Sam on the way to school and asked him if he was down for pulling a senior prank.

We got some window chalk and wrote messages on every single car in the parking lot. I popped my head up for a second and saw the school principal running toward Sam. It turned out that the principal was tipped off by the mail carrier. We were sent home for the day and told that we couldn't walk at graduation unless we cleaned off every car in the lot. I didn't really care about walking at that point, but I knew my parents wouldn't be happy if I didn't. It was a rough way to end my senior year.

Minus some bumps in the road, I got into college. I did it! Things were looking pretty okay. I walked at graduation wearing an enormous gown that made me feel like a baby judge. The gown was almost as big as the anger and fear I had boiling inside of me. Every few minutes during that never-ending ceremony, my eyes pooled with tears. I looked around at all the happy faces of my classmates and proud faces of the families sitting in front of us. I was feeling resentment that my summer was being ripped away from me. The next day I would pack my car and head down route eighty to embark on the first chapter of college: summer school. I couldn't express to you how angry this made me. I had no one to blame but myself.

After the ceremony, we went out to eat with the family and everyone expressed how proud they were. I couldn't help but feel like they were just saying that out of obligation. I packed my bags and went to bed. I tossed and turned all night, consumed by the worry that I was going to inevitably fail college.

CHAPTER 13:

THE STEP AHEAD

AT THAT POINT, I WAS AT A POINT IN MY LIFE where I had no belief in myself; that meant zero confidence. I really didn't know who I was, I didn't know what I was good at, but one thing was for sure: I knew I was bad at school. I drove in complete silence to school. There was no music playing, the windows were up, and my mind just raced. I was terrified. It felt like the shortest forty-five minutes ever. When I pulled in, I saw other students carrying stuff from their cars. There was a big sign that said, Centenary College when I pulled into the campus; something about seeing that sign made it all so real. Everything inside me told me to turn around. Usually my bail-out instinct would have got me out of that parking lot real quick, but for some reason that time I fought back a little and drove in.

My mom and dad were so excited while they helped me unpack. They probably never thought we would be there. Their excitement was starting to anger me, and they could tell I was upset. This was it, the final countdown. My parents were about to leave me in my living nightmare. When everyone did eventually leave, though, I felt so alone. My girlfriend at the time Had given me a Card, and I sat in my room holding it with the door shut and cried. I was trying to keep it quite because I didn't want anyone to hear me. I finally got up, wiped some of my tears real fast, and ran into the bathroom, locking the door behind me. I remember turning the light on, putting my hands on the sink, and looking at myself in the mirror. With tears in my eyes

I said to myself, *Jordan, it's time to change. You cannot let this beat you. You must give it everything you have. You know it will work if you do.*

Now let me explain what this program was all about and how I viewed it when I first got there. The entire day was scheduled for me. Every hour is set up, even bedtime! They even went far as to take our keys (to make sure we weren't going to flee, I suppose. Let's be honest, if I had mine, I might have. This felt like real-life jail. The first night there, while I was lying in bed, I got a phone call from my brother and my best buddy Mike. They couldn't help but bust my chops about how they were on their way to the beach house. I hung up the phone, nearly in a rage. *Why did I have to be the only kid on earth that had to go to summer school to get into college?* In that moment, I almost quit. I thought long and hard about packing my bags right then and there, but then there was that thing about not having my keys. Insert an eye roll here.

Each room was appointed a resident advisor (RA). This person was there to help keep you on track. Basically, they were a personal babysitter. They woke us up in the morning, took us to breakfast, escorted us to our classes, and so forth. These weren't normal classes, and they certainly weren't what I was used to. They were two hours long. Do you know how hard it was for me to sit for two hours?! At the end of the day, the summer-school students had a mandatory three-hour study hall until ten p.m. By eleven, it was lights out. How does that sound for a young eighteen year old, right out of school, during summer break? This was something, however, that I never knew existed. It's called a schedule. It was wildly new to me. I thought they just wanted to ruin my life and make summer school as bad as possible.

Looking back, I can see the big picture. They were trying to instill consistency and diligence. After eight weeks of doing this over and over, something would have to stick, right? Not only was the plan to make consistency a virtue, this routine was set up to change us. I look at it like the educators were coming from one side and the students another, with opposite ideals and opposite worlds. But we were each pieces to a puzzle. Everything had to line up just right in order for big changes to be made. I had the support of my parents and the college. Everyone was rooting for me. I just had to be my own biggest supporter. A few weeks in, my attitude was starting to change as I realized that everyone was on my side and there was a method to this madness. I started to feel uplifted by the people around me, who made me feel good about myself and eager to achieve.

After the pep talk I gave myself about needing to change, I got a little fire inside of me. The first day that classes started, I woke up early, before the RA. I got myself to class—no babysitter needed—and I sat in the front row. That first step made all the difference. I felt smart as soon as I sat down. Now I am going to take you step by step through what was going on in my mind, because I will never forget it. Throughout my previous school years, I sat in class and tried to listen, but I could never understand what the lesson was or what we were learning. I always gave in and just zoned out. I was never prepared, and often I didn't even know when we had a test or an assignment due. So, on the first day I got my front row seat and I pulled out a notebook and brand-new pen. Check, check, check. My eyes were locked on to the teacher's lips. I soaked in every word she was saying, never letting my mind wander.

The first thing the teacher did was hand us a syllabus. I didn't know what that was, but it sounded hard. I saw on the syllabus: test, quiz, test, quiz, test. My heart started racing, and I had that feeling mounting inside me that would always make up want to run and hide. I fought it off like a bad craving and my eyes burned through the syllabus. I said to myself, *Not this time*, and took a deep breath. After leaving that class I was nervous, but I wasn't defeated. I was fighting the little voices in my head that said, *Comfortable, Call your mom, Quit, Go home, Lose focus, It's okay, you have an IEP.* At that point, I knew these were just my excuses, and I had to learn to fight them. I was swiping those thoughts left and right. Regardless of my will to battle the voices, they kept coming at me. It was a full-time job talking to myself and keeping myself motivated.

I was in the business of changing at that point. I went to class every day, I stayed alert every second of the class, and I took down all the notes, even though I couldn't really read my own handwriting. I would try to improve myself by writing as slowly as possible. The truth was that even though my handwriting sucked, just the fact that I was listening and putting in the effort to transfer those thoughts on to paper was helping me. I was learning a lot about myself and the other students in the first few days. Some kids were negative, some had different issues than me, but we all had one thing in common: A lack of confidence in school. For me, though, this was the first time I started to slightly believe in myself; there was a flicker of confidence. I started to follow through with everything I told myself I was going to do. This was a high I never felt before, and I remember thinking, *This is what change feels like.* My attitude toward the program did a 180. This program was everything; it was wonderful. This program was morphing me into the Jordan I was supposed to be.

We had a lot of resources during our time in the program. The three-hour study hall, tutors for every subject, and learning specialists. I utilized them all, which was something I had never done before. I used every single accommodation they had. I was 100 percent focused on changing my life. This is another reason why this program was so great. They equipped the students with the proper safety nets and tools to help us be the best we could be. Every week when I talked to my learning specialist, she always made me feel good and it kept the fire burning. During week two of the program, I passed my first test all by myself. The feeling I got when I saw that passing grade was such a rush. It was a rush to push harder and to be better. I said to myself, *I did this all by myself. All my studying made this happen.* This solidified to me that I was capable to be a college student. So many people along my journey so far had told me that I wasn't made for college and that I wouldn't able to stay above water, let alone achieve. Seeing that grade only strengthened my mission to prove them wrong. I swear I transformed a little faster; I was like the little guy changing into the hulk. My walk became a little different, my eyes became a little more squinted, and I was in tunnel vision to finish this program with all As.

Two weeks into the program, I started to make a name for myself as a good student ... What?! Me, labeled a good student a year ago was crazy, but now it was who I was. I was becoming who I was supposed to be, and truly, it wasn't that I was a good student. It was that I wanted to change and be the best version of myself possible. Here is where I learned that change comes from trying and making the efforts necessary to continue to try every day regardless of the failures that you may endure. My confidence was growing slowly, but increasingly strong. Each day I was laying bricks of confidence, building my foundation. Each brick I laid changed me a little more. I started smiling and feeling good. I didn't even have an outline for the first eighteen years of my life, and now, in two weeks, I had started laying bricks! This was unbelievable to me.

I continued to push forward until the end of the program. As it was coming to an end, I felt like only did I have bricks in place but the success I was feeling was growing roots in me. It's not that being successful in class defined me, but my inner voice and inner self-worth was defining the success I was having in class. *I am now successful in school. I am now holding myself to a certain standard.* I lived up to what I visualized four weeks ago, at the start of the program. I brought my vision to life, and it was the first time I realized that if you want something bad enough and you believe in yourself, you will become obsessed with ensuring that your vision comes to fruition. I was completely obsessed with the success I felt and the success I wanted to continue to achieve. I would sit in the study period, and the assignment I had due by the end of the week was finished in two days. I kept going, I didn't take breaks, I didn't play on the computer, and I didn't talk to the other kids in study hall. I just worked and kept that tunnel vision alive!

CHAPTER 14:

I STARTED TO NOTICE THE CHANGE

I STARTED TO FEEL A LITTLE DIFFERENT. I WAS feeling this success, something that I had never felt before. Students would ask me for help. They would say, "He's smart, he gets it." I remember thinking, *Wow, this girl really thinks I'm smart. I've never had anyone think that way about me.* That feeling was all I ever wanted: to know how the smart kids felt. At that point, I realized that I had to believe that I really was smart, because I was! Teachers started speaking to me differently, and my parents started talking to me like I was an adult. Everything was falling in to place as I continued to secure this foundation. Day by day I would tell myself, *Jordan, stay focused you're almost done, but you need to finish this with a 4.0!* A 4.0 was a far reach from my high school GPA of a 1.7. You have to give me credit for setting the bar high. I focused on this goal every day while doing my schoolwork and laying my bricks. A few weeks before, it was unfathomable that I would be able to achieve a 4.0 GPA, but, upon completion of the program, this goal came to life.

On the last day of the program, we had a picnic to celebrate all of the hard work we had put in. They even gave some awards. I was sitting there on the bench, just minding my own business, not really listening to what was going on, when all of a sudden my name was called. I looked up like, *What?! Me?* I was utterly stunned. The woman giving out the awards said, "Yes. You were the hardest worker and most improved student. Congratulations!" I held that certificate in my hand, beaming, thinking about my first day in the bathroom when I made that promise to myself. That certificate was proof that I was on the right track. When I got back to my room, I called my mom to share the news with her. She shared in my joy and told me she had always believed in me.

Something changed at that moment. I looked at myself a little differently. I saw someone in me that I had never seen before. I saw a superstar in my mind for that one moment as I walked through campus, smiling about everything I had accomplished. This moment was a cornerstone for me. As I reflected on myself, my time in high school, and my time in this program, I realized that I thought I was lacking intelligence when actually I was lacking structure, tools, and, most importantly, determination.

CHAPTER 15:

AND IT BEGINS

IT WAS AUGUST BY THEN, AND I HAD ABOUT three weeks left of summer before I went back to college with the whole student body. That left me three weeks to mentally prepare for one of the biggest fights of my life: myself.

I kept thinking that I was going to forget everything I had learned. The voices were creeping back in to influence me into thinking that I wasn't really prepared for this. My confidence was vanishing. I had just made it through an extremely overwhelming program that was supposed to get me ready for the real deal, but the old, insecure Jordan was still inside me. He wanted to run and hide. I couldn't understand why the old me was trying to break through again. Nonetheless, I knew I had to fight him. I fought him every day. Every time an undesirable thought came to mind, I quickly replaced it with a positive one. I did this over and over. It was exhausting. However, with perseverance and a strong mind, the old Jordan grew tired and the new Jordan grew stronger. I was siphoning out the weaker parts of myself with every internal battle. The new me never got tired; it grew layer upon layer of tough skin until I was bulletproof to any negative thoughts that came to mind.

My first day as an official college student was one of the most intimidating days of my life. I remember getting my schedule, looking at the classes, and feeling my chest get tight. In that instant I bit down on my lip and said to myself, *You are all going down. I will crush these classes like I did in summer school.* I was completely determined to keep my 4.0 GPA as it stood. I worked for it and prayed on it every day. Every night before I went to bed I would say, *Please, God, give me and my family full health, and please help me get good grades in school, please. Amen.*

My first class began with the expectations and the syllabus of the class presented to us. I now knew what a syllabus was, go me! The professor talked about his class and the paper that was due, and how it was 90 percent of our grade. I said to myself, *If that's 90 percent of my grade, I'm in trouble.* Luckily, I knew the secrets to success. I knew that Centenary had tutors available throughout the day that I could fit in between classes. This was something I would never do on my own before, but I was determined to keep my high GPA alive. I needed to prove to myself that I was ready for this.

CHAPTER 16:

THE HIDEOUT

THE FIRST DAY OF SCHOOL BROUGHT FEARS THAT I didn't have to worry about in summer school. The rest of the student body arriving at school meant that I would be subject to everyone finding out about my learning disability. College gave me a clean state, a chance to reinvent myself, which I had started to do during summer school. I wanted to cling to that image of the smart kid. I wanted to keep running with that version of myself, and I desperately wanted to peel away from those feelings of inadequacy and academic segregation I felt throughout high school. So, it's safe to say that I wanted to keep my learning disability under the radar.

During my first official week I had a short paper due, and I was horribly nervous about getting it done. I walked right downstairs to the tutoring center and I asked for an English tutor. At this point I had no friends, and I was very worried that people were going to see me in the tutoring center and I was going to be labeled again. I sat there, nervously looking around for glaring eyes and diminishing looks from others. Then something came to mind. I said, *This is me, and I am going to use the resources that this school has. Screw what anyone else thinks, I am going to be the best Jordan I can be.* Suddenly a weight was lifted off my shoulders. I was free from fear of being judged. I realized I was doing this to improve myself, and there was nothing shameful about that. Self-improvement is life's water, without it we will never grow, never prosper. From that point on, I didn't care about anyone seeing me at the tutoring center. In fact, I made efforts to utilize every academic resource available to me at Centenary, and I mean every one! The resources were put in place to make students better. My attitude changed. *Why didn't everyone utilize these resources?* I no longer felt like the bottom of the barrel with this attitude. I was rising to the top of the barrel with a new vision.

Now this is what everyone reading should understand. The only version of yourself that matters is the version of yourself that you see. Who is looking back at you in the mirror? Is your version defeated, anxious, doubtful, self-loathing, insecure? Do you let others define you? Do you let your negative self-talk run the show? Are you sitting in the tutoring center worrying about who is judging you instead of focusing on your grind? You are the only person who is going to make yourself or break yourself. Read that again. Now, let me explain … when going through school, especially high school, you don't understand that life is so much bigger than your current situation. As kids and young adults, we are too worried about how to fit in: what college you are going to, what sports you play, what clothes to wear, what makes you cool, and who likes you? I hope to smash this idea. I hope to instill in you that none of that is relevant. One day you will awaken from these delusions and you will say, *Wow, I can't believe I put so much emphasis on these things.* Thoughts like these deter us from the potential that we have inside of us and skew our outlook on life, because these thoughts are inconsequential in the long run. If only I had squashed these thoughts in high school, I could have homed in on my focus sooner.

I used to go to bed at night and pray for two things. I would say, *God, please swap my brain out with a new one when I'm sleeping, and please God when I wake up, make me five foot ten.* My prayers were answered; I'm five foot five now, but what I feel when I walk into a room and when I look in the mirror is that I am standing six foot five. My brain is the same old brain, just trained through determination and marinated with self- confidence. When I look back at everything I prayed for, everything I thought God never gave me, I already had it. God bestows on all of us abilities and potential, but it is up to us to awaken and nurture that potential. Before this point in my life, I was selling myself way too short by not taking the efforts to unlock my potential, by letting the minimal expectations others had for me bog me down, by letting my insecurities and negative self-image hold me back. This mindset is dead.

CHAPTER 17:

THE NEW IDENTITY

BY THEN, I WAS MIDWAY THROUGH COLLEGE, and my life had done a complete 360. I single-handedly changed my life at that point, and I started to notice the changes it had on me as a person. When I was younger I would always say to myself, *I hope I am successful*. I was worried about success not being in the cards for me because I thought if I wasn't good at school that meant I had no chance. This is 100 percent not true, and I was finally starting to realize that! What makes you successful is not the ability to turn out a good grade or be a good student, it's the person you become after putting in massive amounts of effort to hit your goals. Because every day I was constantly thinking about my classes, my GPA, the test I had coming up, and subsequently obsessing over it, that train of thought morphed me into the person I was deep, deep down. By making these efforts daily, I was building this foundation for life, and I didn't even know it. I created a standard for myself so high, and my aim was to hit it every single time.

I finally realized that life is all how you look at it, and you can sit there and take it or you can go out there and get what's yours. I started to get what was mine, instead of letting others tell me what I deserved or what I could and couldn't obtain. As I progressed through college, I had no idea what I wanted to do long term. I decided to major in psychology, because I wanted to help kids like me. I thought that this was a good place to start.

CHAPTER 18:

COLLEGE GRADUATION

COLLEGE GRADUATION WAS COMING UP, WHICH
was a day I had never thought was possible! That day was never part of my vision or my plan, until that day I looked myself in the mirror and promised myself I was going to change. I look at Centenary University as a transformation machine. I walked onto campus one person, and by the time I was done I was a totally new Jordan Toma, physically and mentally. *Now that college was ending, what was next? Where to go from here?* I still wasn't sure. My momentum was still high, even though I was petrified about the next step.

I am going to share with you what happens when your life is on the verge of change and what my brain starts to do at this point. I am going to show you how to win during a crucial turning point like this in your life. But before I do, I want to share the most important part of graduation day. Like I said before, when I was graduating from high school I envied all of the smart kids with cords and honors, looking like geniuses. I wanted to look like that, I wanted to feel the pride those kids must have felt. In May 2012, my college graduation day, I put on my black gown just like the one from high school, but I also had a little plastic bag with something extra in it. I had cords! I am just smiling writing this, because I can't begin to explain the pride and joy I felt laying those cords around my neck, walking with honors. I stood tall, wrapped those cords around my neck, and said, *You did it, Jordan.* At that moment, I knew that my vision grew even stronger and I was ready for whatever was going to happen next. Wherever my journey was about to take me, I was ready. When they called my name during the ceremony, I stood six feet tall, shook the college president's hand, and looked out to the crowd at my parents. It was one of the best feelings to date; I was so in love with those cords. We went out to lunch and I took the gown off, but walked into the restaurant with my cords on. I wanted the whole world to know I did it. I, Jordan, graduated with cords and honors, just like one of the smart kids. It was a dream come true.

At that point in my life, I was a college graduate (with cords), feeling on top of the world; I felt like the smartest person that had ever lived. But a new road starts here with a blank slate, with new fears, anxiety, and old memories of all the negative thoughts and feelings that I used to have. Even though I built myself into a more confident version of myself, those anxieties still lingered beneath the surface. It's a scary thing when these anxieties come out to play, because they can paralyze you mentally if you let them. I crushed college and any fears that followed me through that journey, but for this new journey in the real world, my fears thought they could take the reins. I started to think about my competition in the workforce and how they all went to better colleges—whatever that means, because college is who you become while you're there, not where you went in the process, how they are smarter and more worldly. I feared that my competition, my employers, and my colleagues would discover that I had trouble learning, that I had trouble picking up on things right away. *They are going to wonder why this adult man can't spell. They are all going to find out I have a learning disability, and they are going to treat me differently. I came this far and I'm going to let my parents down, I'm not going to be successful, everyone in the room is smarter than me.* Wow, that was a lot of negativity, a lot of insecurities rising to the surface. I had to make a choice in that moment when my fears were trying to cripple me, and if this happens to you this is what you must do: You must get up, look at yourself in the mirror, and remember how far you have come and reflect on the person you became through all the struggle. Let yourself know this is your time to shine, this is what you worked so hard for! That new you is ready to show the world what it takes to be successful! You need to swipe all the negative feelings and thoughts away like mosquitoes on a muggy summer night, like a ninja. You can't let the negative thoughts in, and you must keep talking yourself up! Self-love is vital to success. This tactic and mindset will jump start you past this and any roadblock. This type of roadblock will show up many times in your life. Some stick around longer than others, but your perseverance has to be stronger than that roadblock. With this mentality, you will soar over that barrier every time. Each time you beat that funk, the better and stronger you will get, but you have to keep that positive self-talk up, you have keep that fire lit inside yourself. says, You have to fight like your life depends on it, because it does. I promise you, it does!

CHAPTER 19:

NO MORE COLLEGE, AND NO JOB

IT WAS NOW JUNE 2012, AND I STILL DIDN'T know what my next step was. I decided not to go to graduate school for my masters in social work, which was what my psychology degree set me up to do. I was eager to just start working, but where to start? I kept second-guessing my choice because I felt lost, and the fear of failure was setting in. So I decided to get my nose into the computer and just start applying to as many jobs online as I could. A few days later, I received a call from a very friendly guy from a home remodeling company. Little did I know this was the beginning of a life-changing job opportunity. I had no idea what this job entailed, but as soon as we started talking, I liked the guy on the phone. I liked the way he talked about the job, and I liked what they were offering. He asked if I'd like to set up an interview with the vice president, and I agreed. *Wow, my first big interview, game time!* I got all dressed up, nice tie, shoes, and a suit. I felt good and I felt ready.

I was called in for my interview and the vice president explained that the job was door-to-door sales. My duty in this position would be to sell the appointment. I was a little unsure about what this meant exactly, so I asked, "So I am running around all day door to door, selling windows?"

He said, "Yes! That's it! We put you in a group with a bunch of guys, provide you with a map, and the rest is up to you guys." Then he asked me what my best sales attributes were.

I drew a blank, because I didn't know what attribute meant. I just gazed at him, hoping he would use a different word, wishing I could phone a friend or ask him to use that word in a different sentence. Instead I just said, "What do you mean?"

He said, "Why would you be good at sales?"

I snapped out of the dumbfounded daze, and said, "I've gotten really good at going after things and being determined."

He thanked me and told me that I would get a phone call in a few days to let me know if I got the position for not. I felt so foolish. I got in the car and started punching the steering wheel and cursing at myself for not being able to think of what attribute meant. I really felt like I fudged up my first big shot, and I was really down on myself for it. I drove home, telling myself that I was never getting that job.

When I got home, I immediately hit the computer to send out more resumes because I was sure that I had bombed that interview. A full day went by with no calls about any jobs. All of a sudden, I was in the shower and the phone rang. It was the vice president of the home-remodeling company, and he called to offer me the job. I got nervous at the news and I was half stunned, so I asked him if I could think about it for a day. I took a long shower and pondered the job, getting more and more nervous about the unknown. I had the thought that I was in a sheltered world at Centenary, and now I had to trust that everything I went through was real and useful. Having a learning disability is a very personal situation, everyone handles it so differently, but for me it was all I worried about. I was always comparing myself to other people who didn't have learning disabilities. I saw how they did things and knew that whatever the task was, it was going to be ten times harder for me.

The next day I still hadn't decided on the job, but I knew I wanted to hit the ground running so I went to the gym to clear my head. After my workout, I was getting my bag from the locker room and an older gentlemen who I talked to sometimes asked me how I was doing, so I told him about the job offer I got. I asked him if he thought I should take it. He immediately told me yes, and added me that I would learn a lot doing door-to-door sales. He seemed so sure, he didn't even blink an eye. This encouraged me, and the first chance I got when I left the gym I made the call to the vice president to tell him that I accepted the offer. This endeavor would shape the next five years of my life.

CHAPTER 20:

DOOR-TO-DOOR SALES

IT WAS MY FIRST DAY ON THE JOB. I HAD ON A nice polo shirt, some golf shorts, and sneakers. I was ready to take over the world; it was like the Step Ahead Program all over again. I was scared, but ready to show everyone what I was made of. I revived that same motivation I had in during college, and it was only growing.

It was 11 a.m., and the room started filling up. About fifty guys walked in to look at a big projector of all the numbers of confirmed appointments for the day. Everyone was exposed during these meetings. I saw a lot of threes, twos, and zeroes. The vice president was calling out all of the sales reps with zeroes. I paid close attention to the guys with fours and fives. I decided to make a challenge for myself. I looked for the number-one guy and I said to myself, *I will beat him every time, just let me loose.* I was like a caged animal ready to fight. The meeting wrapped up and it was time to hit the road. Suddenly, one of the guys told me I had to memorize a script to say at the front door for every potential customer. My brain was like, *What?!* It was a page long, and I couldn't go ring doorbells until I memorized it perfectly. This was very hard for me. All of the other new guys seemed to have it down already, and I was only on the first line. My insecurities were rising. I started to feel the sweat beading off my forehead like it used to in school. I was beginning to talk myself out of doing this because it was getting hard. Right there I had to stop and remember why I started. I had to remember that I wanted to change back in 2008. I needed to remember that promise that I kept to myself, the promise that I was going to change no matter what. I had to keep that promise to myself, so I shut down the negative self-talk and began to talk myself back up. I went home that night after reading the paper all day and read the damn thing all night long. I rewrote it over and over because that was the best to make it stick to my brain. I wrote that script down 100 times, and finally I was able to say it word for word. On my thirty-five-minute drive to the office the next morning, I recited the sales pitch over and over. I was ready. I fought through that mini storm and made it out on top. This was another boost of motivation to add to the ride.

I was ready to be let go, to get out on the road, and start selling windows. I had a great manager who always instilled positive energy in me. Before I even started, he would tell me I was going to be great. He would say, "Jordan, you're going to be so good. I can tell." I was kind of questioning his confidence in me, because I was still working on believing in myself. Eli never seemed to let me forget the potential that was inside of me. To this day, I still call him once in a while and we talk about the future. I owe a lot of my successes to this man, who constantly built me up. His words were there when my self-confidence was wavering and this was important during that time in a fresh and intimidating new environment. My first day on the road, I watched the other guys walking door to door so I decided to run to each door. The more people I saw in less time, the more opportunity, right? I ran to every door from noon to eight p.m., and I finished with six confirmed appointments on my first day! I didn't even notice it was eight o'clock and the day was over, I was so focused on selling I could have gone all night. The last sale I got, it started pouring rain while I was giving my pitch. I closed the deal at 8 p.m. in the rain and ran right into the van everyone was going nuts! As we were all heading back to the office, the vice president called my cell. He received live updates of our progress in the field, and he wanted to congratulate me on an impressive first day. It was during this moment that I felt like, for the first time, something came easily to me and all I had to do was be myself. I said, *Jordan, you are on to something!* I sat there thinking about it, and I thought, *Is this what it feels like for the smart kids in school when the teacher puts something on the board and they just know it?* I really started to comprehend that I might have a gift that I really should use. Now, a gift is something that comes naturally and easily for you, but you still have to work hard to use all of its potential. Some people leave their gifts up to the universe and never grow them to what they are meant to be. I decided that I was going to grow this gift and utilize all of my potential, never speculating *What if?*

CHAPTER 21:

STILL SELLING

I WAS GETTING INTO THE GROOVE AFTER A FEW weeks. I established myself as the number-one guy in the office week after week, but I wanted to be the number-one guy in the company. This was the first time in my life that when I walked into a room I felt that I had control of my life and my circumstances. I felt like the kid in math class that knew every answer. I set goals every day, and either hit them or exceeded them. It was a feeling I can't explain, it was a natural high every day to hit my goals. This daily grind was creating the Jordan my mom had told me about, the one she always knew I was capable of being. While I was making enormous strides working for this company and it was doing amazing things for my self-esteem and my brain, I still had no clue what I wanted to do with my life past this job. I just knew whatever I was doing at that current moment I was going to give it whatever it took to be the best I could be. I committed to this mindset after college when I saw what I was capable of, and I carried that mindset into that job. At that point, I felt like anything was possible, even though I didn't know where I was going or how long I would be doing this.

One day on the job stands out to me and strengthened my mindset even more. It was a Friday, and the vice president of marketing was pumping us all up before we hit the pavement. He was going over the numbers and he said, "Who is going to finish number one in the company today? Not our office, the whole company."

I was the only one who raised my hand, and I said, "I am!"

My vice president looked at me and said, "I know you will."

When I made my first step out of the van onto the pavement, I knew I was going to do what I said I was going to do. I hit the ground running, like I always do, like my shoes were on fire, but with a little more spark than usual. I made a promise to the vice president and everyone in that room, and, more importantly, to myself that I was going to finish number one that day.

Monday morning of the following week the numbers came out for Friday, the day I said I was going to set records. *What do you know? I did it!* I finished number one in the company. My vice president said, "Jordan said he was going to finish number one on Friday, and he did!"

Everyone cheered and clapped! Everyone looked at me like some type of machine, like it was impossible, like I had some special powers to be doing what I was doing. I knew that wasn't true, because of what I've been through. I knew I didn't have powers, I knew I had deficits, but I just worked really hard to overcome them. The weird thing was that everyone in the company looked at me like some kind of monster that never failed, that hustled until the end and always finished number one, asking me how I did it. I looked back at them and said, "Hey this is possible. You can do it too, just run side by side with me and I promise you will make it happen!" The cool thing was that I started to inspire other people in my van, the guys who were on the same route as I was. They started to go to the gym like me every morning, they started to bring their own lunch like me, they started to jog door to door instead of walk. Everyone was getting better, working harder, and I ignited that! It felt so good to be the example, to be the person that other people wanted to be, to have abilities that others envied.

CHAPTER 22:

LEVELING UP

Eventually I was invited to move to a dif-ferent part of the company because of my success with the door-to-door sales. My outlook really started to change at this point. I was asked to move to the retail aspect of my job. In this area of sales, the job is to walk around a wholesale store and sell window appointments to shoppers. Think about it, you're walking around a big store trying to buy food, household items, and so on, and I walk up and stop you in your tracks. I had to get the shoppers interest and attention long enough to get on the phone, answer nine questions, and confirm an appointment for a salesman to come to their house. That was an insane task, even more challenging and intimidating than walking (running) up to people's houses. I was assigned to be at the store from 11 a.m. to 8 p.m. They told me if I got five confirmed appointments before 8 p.m. I could leave, but nobody ever did this so they weren't worried. That was a big mistake on their part.

I was totally up for the task. I had *Five appointments by one o'clock in the afternoon* as my goal. I walked in the store everyday for two weeks and had five appointments set up by 1 p.m., and then I would go home because I maxed out the bonus. I really started to uncover how the mind works when you put it to a task. I started to realize if I 100 percent believed in myself no matter what the task, I was sure to accomplish it, even if no one had done it before me! Once I realized this, I leveled up.

After two weeks in this position, my bosses called me in and changed the bonus plan because I was making too much money and only working for three hours a day. So, if you are reading this and you're down in the dumps and you really don't think you can do something, you have to take a deeper look inside yourself. You don't know what you can do until you start to believe and take action. It's not magic or luck or talent, it's leveling up. That's all I did! In the past, whenever I would have doubts about a task or about myself, I would give up, or run and hide from the task. I did this for the first eighteen years of my life. This isn't living. This is called complacency. At eighteen, I started living. I started to level up, day by day, week by week, month by month, and year by year. If you recall, when I took that job I had no idea what I was doing, and after a short time they had to change their pay parameters based on my achievements. I had everyone looking up to me; I was giving advice. More important than the money and the accolades, I had confidence. This journey just goes to show that when something new comes your way, something that scares you, being uncomfortable is a natural feeling, but that doesn't mean you run from it. In fact, you need to run toward that uncomfortable feeling or that fear, and trample it. Embrace being uncomfortable; it can change your life in a big way or in a bunch of small ways that may lead to something great.

CHAPTER 23:

TIME TO MOVE ON

WHILE I REALLY ENJOYED MY JOB AS A WINDOW and home improvement salesman, I felt like I was outgrowing it. This was a very uncertain time in my life because I knew this job wasn't the end game, but I didn't know where to go from there. I was still searching for what it was that I loved to do. I knew I loved talking to, meeting, and helping people. Ideally, I wanted to find something that encompassed all three. Ultimately, I decided to leave the window company and apply to work at an insurance company.

My father was with this insurance company for many years, and when I told him I wanted to go for it he said, "It's not the same anymore, it's too hard!" I remember just looking at him blankly after he said that. He kept shaking his head, saying, "It's not the same," over and over again. This really got me mad. He was basically saying I couldn't do it. Even though he was discouraging me, he told me to try anyway.

That night I decided to leave the window company. When I told the vice president of sales that I was going to start a new job at the insurance company, he tried to talk me out of it. It felt good to be wanted; he knew he was losing a solid employee. Ultimately, he told me he was sad to see me go, but he knew I will be successful at the insurance company just as I while working for him. This meant a lot to me. He told me I was successful, and he saw success for me in the future. The one thing I had worried about my whole life, being successful. To hear the words come out of someone else's mouth made me really feel like I was on my way. All that time in high school, feeling like I would never amount to anything because I was in modified classes, and there I was sitting across from a company vice president who was telling me he knew I would be successful.

When I got home, my dad said it was time to study. *Study?!* My face went white with fear. He said, "Jordan, you have to pass three tests before you can sell insurance. The first two aren't bad, but the third one is a hard. I'm not going to lie." I was panicking. I kept asking my dad if he'd ever seen anyone fail all three tests. My mind went right back to 2007, when I felt so small. It was now 2013, I was twenty-three years old, I had overcome so much, but there I was, feeling miniscule again. I was nervous, and it was all I could think about. I told myself I was going to work but I didn't know the financial industry, I didn't realize what I was getting into, and my paranoia about these tests was taking over. I have learned, however, that when the mind is busy it's best to put it to work, so I signed up for a class that next week, and I had two days to talk myself out of the self-doubt. *Game face time.*

CHAPTER 24:

STUDY TIME

THE FUNNY THING ABOUT LIFE IS THE JOURNEY prepares you for all of the unknown events ahead, and you don't realize it until afterward. The best way to work your way through the unknown is to get yourself in unconformable situations that you know are going to test you. When you fight through those obstacles, more weapons are added to your arsenal when it's really time to go to battle. When I say weapons, I am talking about mental weapons. Your mind is the ultimate weapon, an arsenal that has to be equipped for battle at all times. The only way to stock your arsenal is to continually challenge it throughout your journey. This requires you not to take shortcuts or handouts. Your journey consists of just you versus what you are really made of.

When I sat in the insurance classes, my eyes were glued on the teacher. I tried to channel the focus that I had on my first day of summer school at Centenary. My laser focus was being crushed, however, because I just didn't understand the information. I was watching everyone get it, and that brought back to eighth grade in a matter of seconds. I sat there, frustrated because everyone else was getting it but me. I felt small and alone, like the whole world was swallowing me. The real world was mean and unforgiving; there were no tutors after class, no extra credit, no help time, just me and those books. That is when I realized life is made of you versus what you are made of. Life is a battle of will, and I was not able to let those books or the old Jordan beat me out of a good future. I told myself this. I said, *Let's get through class, then at the library I will re-read and re-write all of this and I will understand it.*

I had to get creative and figure out a way that I knew would work for me. My plan was to do this every day: go to class, get through it, and crush the information at night, alone, in my zone. Page by page, practice question after practice question, I re-wrote the questions and the answers over and over until my hand went numb from morning to night! I did this for one week straight until I was ready to take the state test. I was extremely nervous, feeling like I needed to prove this to myself and to my dad.

Test number one was the life-insurance exam. I woke up at 6 a.m. and paced back and forth in my room, re-reading questions in my head. My test was scheduled for 9 a.m., but I showed up at the test center an hour early. My heart was pounding, and all the while, I prayed to God that I wouldn't forget anything. I asked the exam proctor if I could start the test early since I was there, and I think this worked to my advantage because it was just me in that room with no one to compare myself to. I only had myself in that room to battle with. I had earplugs, a pencil, a computer screen, and the will to succeed. *Showtime.* I hit the start button and was flying through questions, feeling better with each passing one. The test had a tool to mark questions you weren't sure of, but I didn't use it once. For the first time in my life I felt pretty good on this test. I was shocked! I finished the exam, closed my eyes, and when I opened them, the word Passed was blinking brilliantly on the screen. No score, just Passed. I smiled so hard, and walked out feeling like a million dollars. All of that hard work paid off.

Feeling great, I called my dad and he said, "You passed??" He was shocked for sure, but he congratulated me. After about ten minutes of extreme bliss, I realized it wasn't over. I had two more tests to take, and the health insurance exam was only a week away.

CHAPTER 25:

ROUND TWO

FOR THE HEALTH INSURANCE EXAM, I REPEATED the same study process as before, but this one wasn't sticking. I felt much less confident walking into this test, and the results showed. I took the test and failed. This hurt. I studied so hard. The information required for these exams isn't exactly the most riveting material, so it was hard to stay engaged. Nonetheless, I kept on plugging away. I hated the feeling of failing so much. Just writing about this failure, I am reliving that pain all over again. I failed, but I took it on the chin and that day I hit the books again. I re-wrote every practice test again until my hands went numb. I never took a break for a week straight and reset my test date. It was round two, second time sitting for the health insurance exam. I showed up early, worked through the test, and failed again. My eyes filled up with tears and anger welled up in my chest. I got up and the woman at the desk handed me a blue paper that said Failed! I walked out to the car with steam between my ears. I couldn't believe this happened two times in a row. All those hours of studying, and I was defeated again. As down and frustrated as I was, I wasn't going to let this failure get in my way. I put in another week of studying. There was no time to waste sulking. I was re-writing answers, working through practice tests, flipping note cards, and I even had my dad quizzing me every night. I wasn't going to fail again. I set a third test date and was ready to go. I walked in, took the test, and failed again, by five points this time. I saw the fail page and squeezed the mouse as hard as I could. I got in the car, called my mom and dad, and just yelled into the phone. *Three times!*

Remember, though, it's not over until you quit and I wasn't prepared to quit. I failed three times in a row, but I wasn't giving up. It was getting tough to keep my confidence up after these repeated blows, and the studying was tedious and draining. The information still didn't feel like it was sticking, regardless of my tireless efforts.

I set my test date once again, but the only available test center was an hour away from where I lived. I had no choice. I knew one thing: that day I was going to have a happy hour-long ride home or a sad hour-long ride home. I woke up at 5 a.m. and drove the hour away, arriving early as usual. I sat in my car and went over all of my notes and filled my head with positivity while I waited for the testing center to open. At 7 a.m., the proctor arrived and he let me in. We talked for a little and I told him that I had failed this test three times already, but this time I was going to pass! He seemed confident that I was going to pass, too, so that made me feel good. He let me in early, around 7:45 a.m. I sat down at my computer for the fourth time, same test, there we were. I passed! Finally, four tries and a million hours of studying later, and I passed. It's only over if you quit people, so never ever quit! I felt like a million bucks, smiling from ear to ear. It was such a great feeling, to see the fruits of my labor pay off, to know that I wouldn't be there happy as a clam, if I gave up the first, second, or third time I failed. I was nervous along the way for sure, but I never doubted myself.

CHAPTER 26:

THAT WAS THE WARM-UP

TWO TESTS DOWN, BUT IT WAS ONLY THE BEGINning. I still had to pass the mother of all tests. This test had been haunting me ever since I knew I had to take it. I felt like I mentally went through war already, but it was not over. My dad told me that as soon as I was hired, the clock started and I had to pass the tests. I didn't want to apply until I was ready for the test, as I didn't need more pressure. It was going to take me six months to prepare for this test. Again, the material was extremely hard to stay engaged with, and it presented a number of obstacles for me. First, it's mind numbingly boring Second, I can't read or understand the terms. Third, I don't know what's going to be on the test. Fourth, I couldn't pronounce or understand the vocabulary.

I took my first practice test and got a 23 percent, and that was trying.

We had a group of seven people in my class studying for the test. The first assignment was to read the entire book. It took me weeks to finish the book, and I didn't remember one thing I read, nor did I understand what I was reading. It was torture. I kept failing every practice test by a large amount; I wasn't even close. I felt like this was going to be impossible. One night I was in my room studying and had just failed another practice test. My mom called me down for dinner and I threw the book on the table.

"I just don't understand!"

My dad looked at my mom and said, "Maybe he can't do it! Maybe it's too hard for him."

My mom took a softer approach, encouraging me that I could indeed do it. I piled my food in, went back to my room, and told myself I could do it. From there on out, I made my mind up to study every second until I was ready. I thought about how far I had come, the Step Ahead Program and all the hard work I put in to finish college with honors. I thought about it all! I said, *I am not going to let this test stop me and all the progress I have made. I didn't go through all this and come this far to stop here.*

Every day after that I woke up at 5 a.m., went to the gym, came home, made eggs and oatmeal, and hit the books by 8 a.m. I studied until 9 at night for six months straight. My dad and mom started to worry about me. They said I was obsessed, and I needed to take a break. I mean it when I say I took zero breaks. My dad went from saying I couldn't do it to saying I was too obsessed. Five months had gone by at this point, and I still hadn't passed a practice test, but I stayed positive. I had to keep the positivity flowing in order to combat any negative thoughts that wanted to bring me down. Remember, self-love is a powerful ally. Every morning I showered and said, over and over, *Jordan, you're going to pass this test.* Six months had gone by at that point, and I finally set my test date. I had two weeks.

I was on a serious mission. My friends called me, asking me to join them at the lake house or the beach, and I continually turned them down, replying, "I have to study."

They would say, "Jordan, you have been studying for a year!!! What if you fail?! Will we ever see you again?"

I said, "No, because I will still be studying. I will not fail!"

I sacrificed a lot of fun trips and memories with friends to profit from the long-term goal. The only mission on my mind was passing this test. My parents were right. I was obsessed. I had tunnel vision like when I was in the Step Ahead Program; I was making it out, one way or another.

I still hadn't passed any practices test up to that point. Six months of my nose in the books, and not a single passed practice test. Right before you take the real test, they give you an official practice exam that basically tells you if you are going to pass or not. I took this exam and I failed. That meant I would probably fail the real test, but in my mind I was not failing. I went through every question, every sentence, and re-wrote the question and answer by hand over and over again until I couldn't feel my hand. I had to move to different parts of the house because I was going crazy. I would switch from my bedroom, to the basement, to the kitchen. I was going stir-crazy, but I kept at it.

So far, the best score I had gotten on a practice test was a 68 percent. This was better than where I started, but not good enough. A 70 percent or better was needed to pass the test. I failed eleven thousand practice tests, but I was still focused and still positive.

I woke up the morning of the test at 5 a.m., sick to my stomach. I went downstairs and tried to eat, but my stomach revolted. My test was set for 8 a.m. My dad offered to drive me and wait in the parking lot. The ride to the testing center I sat quietly, telling myself, *Today is the day,* over and over again. My dad wished me good luck, and I walked in. When I checked in, they took everything I had and put it in a locker. I was escorted to a computer where I was left to put everything on the line. All I had were earplugs and everything I worked for. I hit start on the screen and my heart skipped a beat. It was go time. I started reading the first question and I had never seen it before, so that shook me. I pushed through until I was at question number forty-five. I felt so confused, and I couldn't understand the questions. I was worried, and I was giving up mentally. I got up and went to the bathroom, desperately needing a breather. The last time I went to the bathroom in this state of mind, I promised to change my life. This time, I looked at myself, threw water on my face, and said, *Jordan, you know this. Go pass that test!* Something came over me after that. I walked back in and picked up where I left off in a completely new state of mind. It was like I was in a rhythm. I was moving from question to question and answering everything without second-guessing myself. I flew through the last sixty questions until I finally finished the test. It took ten seconds for the test to grade itself, ten seconds that felt like ten hours.

Boom! Eighty-three percent, I passed! I put my arms in the air, embracing victory, and smiling from ear to ear. It was the best feeling I had ever had. It was over, I did it! I ran out of the testing center toward my dad's car, waving the passing paper in the air. The smile on my face gave it away instantly. I called my mom from the car; she screamed with joy.

Most people won't understand why everyone was so happy in this moment, but if they knew how hard that test was for me, they would understand too. This experience was an eye-opener for me. I asked myself, *What else can you accomplish?* I answered, *Anything! Everything is within reach, I'm coming for everything.*

CHAPTER 27:

A NEW LIGHT, IT'S MY TIME

IT WAS LIKE SOMEONE HAD JUST LET THE ANImal out of its cage; I was completely transformed. The cool thing about life is that you can keep getting better. Every time I thought it was done or I made it through something hard, I saw myself change. I thought I had limits, and now I know there is no such thing. I am free from any negative thought that used to limit me. This was the start of a new journey, where it was time to yet again level up. This is an important part about the journey in life. Sometimes when you're going through something hard, you feel as though you've hit your limit. What you don't realize when you're going through it is that those hard times are forcing you to level up. When you hit the goal, it's not the goal that's important. It's who you've become while reaching it.

I was officially licensed to sell insurance, and I was ready to go. I did the same thing I did at the window company. I looked at everyone and watched the people who were making things happen and I told myself, *You can do this, and nothing is going to stop you.*

I decided after studying for all those tests that I didn't care what happened or who came through those doors, no one was going to outwork me. *I will be the first one there and the last one to go home every day. I will do this 365 days a year. Let's see where that takes me.* Now, let me make something clear. In the insurance industry you will pass all these tests, but you can do a lot of different things and focus on the areas that you like. I am considered a financial advisor, but my main job is to sell life insurance. Selling life insurance is a little different than selling windows.

First, I'm calling people on the phone. Second, I am selling something that is intangible, that can't be seen or used directly. Third, they must pay for it as long as they live.

What really separates selling life insurance from windows is that it's way more important, and I truly believe that. To start, my higher-ups gave me a list of people to start calling, so I did. I booked appointments, but I had to go out with other reps before I could go out alone. I went out with one rep and I sat there, not saying a word, and I watched. I counted fives times where he could have set the policy up, but he missed the boat. I couldn't believe it! He was missing the opportunity left and right.

I believe we all have gifts, and it's our job to discover what they are and how we can use them to help make the world a better place. After about five appointments, I realized what I had that came easy and what others might struggle with. Number one, I found it very easy to connect with a person right away and have them open up with me. Number two, I really cared. I felt for every person I spoke to, and I always treated them as if they were my family. Because I treated people this way, I got the same treatment in return. Number three, as that was the most important part of the job, they have to like me. I had to smile and really love the people I was talking to, because people will see that. I loved meeting new people. I just loved the fact that I was walking into someone's house and we were about to become friends; that was awesome for me. That was always my first step, let's just be friends and we'll see what happens next, and I loved that part of the job.

The first few appointments I had I was just warming up. I remember it was September when I had my breakthrough. I was booked solid for a week, and I kept booking and booking. I sold a policy every day for thirty days. I was so excited with the gains I was making, and it was another eye-opener for me. This is yet another point in my life where I leveled up. I told myself I was the best life insurance agent in the universe. My dad couldn't believe it and my mom was shocked, but they were so proud! I was proud, too, and excited for what was next to come.

CHAPTER 28:

WHAT I'M MADE OF

I STARTED TO GET THE HANG OF THIS INSUR-ance-selling thing. The years were flying by and, before I knew it, I had a little business on my hands. I started making a name for myself. I won every award or contest that was on the radar. In my first full year, I finished second in the country for the entire sophomore sales crew. I also picked up a lot of haters along the way. I never had that happen before, people hating me. In the beginning of my journey, everyone was so willing to help me, but when I started doing well everyone seemed to be against me. I could feel this energy in the office; it was an odd feeling. I'll never forget one time I was standing downstairs in the office talking to a friend of mine, and another rep walked by us and rolled his eyes.

I said, "What was that for?"

He said, "That guy thinks they are feeding you good leads that are ready to go." I was floored! That made no sense to me, and I was so offended. I was the first one there and the last one to leave every night! I started to let it get to me, that this is what people were thinking, that I didn't work for everything I have. The proof was in the pudding, and how could anyone think otherwise?

One day I saw a quote that spoke to me, "If you don't have haters, you're not doing it right." This really sank in, and I stopped caring what everyone else thought. I just kept working, grinding, doing me, and I let the haters continue doing their thing. I said to myself, *I don't care what anyone thinks.*

I'm going to keep working! I learned one thing early on: Most people won't put the extra effort in to be great, most people will try and bring you down, most people won't be happy when you're winning, but that's okay. You have to smile for yourself!

Before I transformed my mindset, I used to ask myself why so many people disliked me, *Why was this happening? I'm a nice guy, a good guy, I work hard.* I understand now. You can't please everyone. You have to keep your vision strong and focus on where you want to go. I put a lot of emphasis on focusing on where you want to go, and the importance of this tunnel vision, but the funny thing was I didn't really know where I wanted to go. What I did know was that I had to keep the pace up. I had to keep working hard, so hard, every day, no days off! I had to keep getting better and improving myself.

There was one rep I worked with, he was about five years in, and one day he said, "Jordan, you are going to burn out. You can't keep this pace up. Trust me, you can't."

An amused smile curled around my lips and I said, "Watch me."

He is no longer with the company. Most of the time, people will put limits on you, but that's because those are their limits. They can't imagine what it's like to break ceilings, and because of that they never will. You have so much more in you, way more then you even know; just keep pushing yourself, and you will transform into a superhero.

CHAPTER 29:

HATERS

THE HARDEST PART ABOUT FINDING YOURSELF isn't always what you think, or at least it wasn't for me. You would think that overcoming your own demons and deficits would be hard enough. There came a point where I was able to laugh at my deficits, but the haters were tough. People are ruthless. People will be out for you, ready to stick their foot out and hoping you trip. Haters are all around us. They hate the people who are winning, the people who are glowing, the people that are figuring it out. They want to figure themselves out so badly, but they fail, and doing so causes them to harbor all this anger and hate for themselves. Unfortunately, that hate needs an outlet. So where does the hate go? To you, the hard worker, goal achiever; they are out to get you and to discredit your success.

Now what should you do about it? Nothing. Keep working and learning, keep figuring out what you are made of and who you are. The harder you push, the more they will show up. They will sit and watch, fixing all of their energy on your downfall instead of on their own game. Let them enjoy the show. They wish they could be doing what you're doing, they dream about it, but it's too scary for them. Not for you, though. You are a goal getter.

Haters come with the life you choose. If you choose a life that is easy, safe, no pushing back, then you won't have to worry about the haters. If you have them, though, you're on the right road. People will love you and people will hate you. Some people will love you to your face and hate you behind your back, but that's okay! You have to love yourself and that is it! Love yourself, be your best friend, and be your biggest fan. That is how you win friends! If you love yourself that much, there is nothing you won't do to make yourself happy and you will meet all of your goals head on.

Another thing: never forget why you started. Keep your eyes on the target at all times! The weather will get wild, but do not take those eyes off the target. At one point, I let the haters get to me. I almost didn't want to do as well just so everyone would calm down. I almost diminished myself to quiet the haters! Can you believe this, considering doing less than you are capable of because your success makes others unhappy? I quickly snapped out of this train of thought. I wouldn't give in to other people because they gave up on themselves. I decided in 2008 to save myself. I have a different type of fire; my motivation is to save myself! Remember that you have to save yourself because no one is going to save you. Maybe your family or a few good people might have your back, but at the end of the day it's on you! You got this. You have control, not bring it on!

CHAPTER 30:

MY KRYPTONITE

I WAS THREE YEARS INTO SELLING INSURANCE, and the momentum was really starting to pick up. I could feel the change in my veins. I was off to a good start in this business, both financially and personally. I was learning how to deal with the haters for the first time in my life and I was navigating the pressures of just being an adult. I knew that if I just kept my head down and kept working, nothing could stop me. Working 365 days a year, no one could catch me. Working day in and day out was allowing me to see the fruition of all my hard work.

After years of self-doubt, perpetual fear, and multiple failures, the dust was starting to settle. My whole life I had been searching for the real me, the one I knew was always there. I just had to reach in and pull him out. I used to pray every night to be successful and to get good grades in school. I never missed a night praying to God to grant me these gifts. As soon as the dust settles, you know the journey is just getting started, because the fight's not over there. You made it through the first few hurdles, but get ready because life is coming to punch you in the face.

When the dust did settle for me, I felt like I could breathe a little and ride the wave. I thought the hardest was over. Then I thought to myself, *If I want to keep growing, there are going to be more hurdles.*

With the business that I was in, there was an opportunity to purchase a pre-existing business. I was kind of new to the business, but I wasn't new to taking risks. It was a huge risk, and at twenty-five years old, writing a check for $100,000 was kind of scary. I had saved everything I could for the past few years, and I was thinking about giving it up. *Was it going to be worth it?* I pondered this for a while, but ultimately I decided that regardless of what happened I would learn from it and grow from it. I decided to take the plunge and buy the business. But there was one more thing to have to do: I had to pass another test.

I know what you're thinking, *Are the tests ever going to end?* I know I felt the same way. First was the series 65 test. This test would allow me to label myself as a financial advisor. Knowing how difficult testing is for me and the great lengths of preparation it takes to overcome a test, I gave myself eight months for this test. So the studying began. I failed practice tests over and over and over again. I said, *Okay, I need a tutor.* I spent 190 bucks an hour and drove an hour to this tutor. I realized that if I kept using this tutor I would have spent all of my money and only be halfway through the book, so that stopped after three weeks.

It was back to the lonely grind. I was alternating between the kitchen, the coffee shop, the bedroom, and the basement. Regardless of the venue, I kept failing. I failed eleven thousand practice tests! I started to look up things online to see what would help me retain information, hoping to gain any advantage. I read that deodorant has aluminum in it and aluminum blocks your memory, so I stopped using that ASAP. I also read that blueberries help improve your memory, so I went out and bought baskets of blueberries. There I was, I never wore deodorant and all I ate was blueberries. You can imagine what I looked and smelled like. I'm surprised my girlfriend at the time stayed with me, but she did (thankfully). So, I was eight months into studying and I decided it was time to sign myself up for the test.

In November 2015, I walked into the testing center, sat down, and I started the test. I was feeling good, but when you're feeling too good, it's an issue. A healthy level of nerves is never a bad thing. I was on the last question, trying to stay focused. I was trying my best not to switch up sentences and words in my head, all the while in the back of my mind I was thinking that I never wanted to have to do this again. I finished the last question, and the test then gives you an option to go back and change answers if you like. I had no patience. I didn't even think twice about it, I just clicked finish. Fail. I was two questions short. I needed ninety-four correct answers to pass, and I got ninety-two correct. My eyes filled up with tears and I walked out hanging my head. I got in my car and saw all the text messages I had gotten, wishing me good luck. I started to cry. I wanted to turn right back around and take it again, but I couldn't. I had to wait thirty days to take it again. I drove home, called my parents, and let them know I had failed. They told me to shake it off and next time I would crush it. I said to myself, *I do have it next time!* No time to feel down, I had to keep climbing.

I walked into my parent's house, went straight up to my room, threw out my deodorant, grabbed a handful of blueberries, and started a 250-question practice test. I said to myself, *Jordan! You will not fail this again. You have thirty days to get it right, baby. Let's do this!* I took that practice tests and ate blueberries for thirty days straight, not leaving my room. I also signed up for a two-day class in New York City to gain some more knowledge about the test. Finally, when I was feeling ready, I booked my test for December 22, 2015, at 9:00 a.m. I got there at 6:30 a.m. and I waited until they opened the doors at 7 a.m.

I said, "My appointment is at nine, but I have to start it now." My heart was thumping violently and my hands were sweating. This was the day to prove to myself that I can do anything I put my mind to. It wasn't only that this test was on the line. It wasn't just about being labeled a financial advisor. My heart, soul, and pride were also on the line. Click, click, click, next, next. As I was answering the questions, I was talking to myself, *Jordan, you got this, you know this* click, next. One hundred-thirty questions later, I was done. I clicked finish. I saw Pass flash across the screen! Remember, I needed to get ninety-four questions correct to pass, and I got exactly ninety-four!

Jordan Toma is the smartest man alive!!!!! I called my dad and I screamed, "I passed! Seventy-two percent on the nose!"

He said, "Get the hell out of there before they change it on you!" Funny guy memory. I laughed, I smiled, I yelled with pure joy. Right there, a new Jordan was born. After everything I went through to pass this test, a new me was made during that process. I'm dangerous!

CHAPTER 31:

I FEEL FREE

AFTER YEARS OF FEELING TRAPPED AND CON-
fined by a label, I am finally starting to feel free. At this point, I have not
only survived but crushed every single scary moment in my life. At the end
of 2015, I had passed every test I needed and purchased a business to boot.
The funny thing that was no matter how many things I achieved, I still had
this worry, this flicker of fear bringing me back to sixth grade. This worry
lingers in front of all my dreams and goals. In a way, I almost think it's the
fire that keeps me going. I am constantly running from that worry, running
in a good way, running toward greatness. My worry can't catch me, I'm
too fast, too motivated. I also feel that worry keeps reminding me of who
I was, and how I thought about myself at the height of my hard times. This
reminder kept pushing me to work past my struggles and that this fight is
nobody's but my own.

It's important to remember you aren't free until you are free of your
own thoughts. Your mind can control every single thing you do. If there is
anything you have learned after reading this story, it should be about the
power of your mind. At this point, I feel like I am outgrowing my own skin,
in a way. I feel the old Jordan is finally being shed. I have made it, and I'm
not done here. I have built myself up to a point where I feel like I need to
share what I have been through. I had to desire to be the person I needed
when I was younger, so I could help students out there who were like me. I

never had that person to look up to when I was going through my toughest times. I felt like having someone to connect to in real life, so I could know this person struggled and worried about the same things I do would be valuable for students like me. I wanted to act as a beacon of hope. I wanted to show students how I made it through the muck and how they can too. This felt like my true calling. All this time throughout my journey, crushing tests, selling windows, selling insurance, and chasing success, I was still searching for what it was that I truly loved. I feel like my journey was setting me up for this, for all of you. I wanted to make it my mission to share my path and to set others students free from the limits of their minds and their disabilities. My whole life I put a limit on my future because of the way I saw myself, compared to others. After all the hard work and positive self-talk, I am ready to truly live.

I have learned many things throughout my life thus far. My biggest takeaway from all of this is that we all our blessed with gifts, but it is up to you alone to uncover just what they are and master them! To do this, you have to keep trying. Failure is not an option. It's only over if you give up. You have your best interest in yourself, and always trust your gut!

CHAPTER 32:

I'M JUST A KID WITH AN IEP

AT THIS POINT IN MY LIFE, I HAVE FINISHED second in the country twice with the most life applications, qualified for every life conference since I started, and I am an eight-time Million Dollar Round Table qualifier. I also have a growing real estate portfolio and an unstoppable mindset. While this all sounds really cool, none of those things mean anything to me. What holds the most value to me is passing those tests and the tenacity it took to get to this point. Most of all, and most importantly, I have delivered myself to a point where I can be an example for every student out there who feels like they aren't smart, or who feels like everyone else is so much smarter than they are. For the student who gets called on in class to read and shakes in fear, who gets nervous about messing up all the words while people laugh at them, for the person who, no matter how hard they're trying, they just can't pronounce the words before them. For the students who gets a test and reads the questions and, no matter how hard you studied you just can't remember the correct answers." For the students who can't concentrate, can't understand, and can't absorb the information. For the parents who were told by teachers, psychologists, and administrators that your child can't ever go to a four-year college or go out and be a successful individual in this world. For every student who wishes and prays that they could be smart, for every single student who carries a label on them they just want to rip off. For every parent and student pleading for God to answer their prayers. Listen to my story and get inspired; go out and write your own story! I know you all have it in you. I promise you do. That is exactly why I wrote this book and that's why I started, I'm Just A Kid With An IEP, LLC, because I needed who I am now, to walk into my school when I was younger.. Now I will be that person for someone else.